"William Cleary's *In God's Presence* is not just another how-to-pray book. Grounded in solid theology, it is at the same time an imaginative—one might even say 'serendipitous'—approach to individual and group awareness of and response to God's presence. I wish it had been available for the course on spirituality I taught this past semester, especially for the way it introduces the reader to the practice of centering. It would be an excellent companion book to Tony de Mello's *Sadhana.*"

Bernard Cooke
Author, *Sacraments and Sacramentality*

"Signs of God's presence among us are justice, peace, and love. So is creativity, since the first we know of God is as one engaged in creativity. *In God's Presence,* by Cleary's creativity, brings the fortunate reader into God's presence! I found delightful the fresh and creative style by which he seduces the reader into the ancient art of prayer. This book is global-catholic in its religious inclusiveness, and playful in his 25 light-hearted beasts and bugs prayers. The humor in these rhymed prayers are good medicine for the humility so necessary for any truly good spirituality. If you need to give your prayer life a shot of zeal and new life, I recommend *In God's Presence.*"

Edward M. Hays
Shantivanam House of Prayer

"When you don't feel like praying, but maybe wish that you did, open this book anywhere, and start. Something good will happen.

"So practical, so profound; so funny, so poetic; so wise with all the traditions of the ages, so contemporary; so very human."

Quentin Quesnell
Professor in the Humanities, Smith College

IN GOD'S PRESENCE

Centering Experiences for Circles and Solitudes

WILLIAM CLEARY

TWENTY-THIRD PUBLICATIONS
Mystic, CT 06355

Twenty-Third Publications
185 Willow Street
P.O. Box 180
Mystic, CT 06355
(203) 536-2611
800-321-0411

ISBN 0-89622-608-5
Library of Congress Catalog Card Number 94-60477
Printed in the U.S.A.

Dedication

With thanks to Roddy, my inspiration...
What a creation you are, my love!
You lighten my heart,
You center me,
I love you.

Contents

IN GOD'S PRESENCE

Introduction

In God's Presence is more than a prayer book. It is an invitation to a simple kind of communication with God called Centering, a communication that may involve every aspect of our lives and everything we do and say. It is an invitation to experience one way of responding to the mystery of God's presence and to know the wonder, the joy, the ecstasy, even the whimsicality—as well as the pain, the turmoil, and the passion of God's Mysterious Presence.

When we use a word like centering, we are trying to name an activity we all do from time to time, but one that we seldom name. Centering is like focusing, except that focusing implies concentrating on something, and centering is not so logical or limited. I vividly remember going to the plays that my two sons were in during their school days. From the moment the curtain opened I was always intensely alert—whether I wanted to be or not—waiting for my child to appear. I was centering. Once Tom or Neil was on stage, I began focusing on them, even if, for the moment, they might not be at the center

1

of the scene. It was just part of being who I was, a mildly irrational parent.

"I don't think centered and focused are synonyms," says Fred Mish of Merriam-Webster. "Focused means something more like 'intent,' 'concentrated,' and it seems more often to refer to a temporary condition than to a continuing state of mind and soul, as centered does."

Mish gives an example from a William Faulkner novel in 1957 in which he describes a character involved in "all sorts of things that would have made a weaker or a less centered man blanch and falter, but not him."

Centering, being centered, makes us strong somehow. It's an act of concentrating on our inner essential self with all its primary connections, and setting aside all the concerns on our edges.

Centering, I would say, is the essential act of prayer: One sets aside all peripheral and immediate concerns and centers one's self on one's center, wherever that is thought of as being: the mind, or the heart, or the breathing. And each of these three centers produces a different kind of centering.

KINDS OF CENTERING *Centering in the heart*—how we feel, and feel about the important connections in our lives—is the most important. Our feelings are at the core of our selves, and once we know our feelings, we know ourselves—and God—for we receive our selfhood moment by moment from the Creating Mystery. Like flowers budding from their center, we are most connected to God in our hearts and feelings.

Centering in the mind is useful also, but it may not connect us immediately to God. It is apt to be theoretical, abstract, and to that extent unreal, even deluded.

Centering in the breathing is also useful, but it is a less ambitious prayer style, therapeutic and relaxing, but not deeply relational. I find it more a psychic bath, refreshing, cleansing, but less than a prayer.

Centering, I believe, is the essence of prayer. And prayer is popular. Religion researcher Michael Hout found that 40% of Americans in their 20s say they pray daily, and another 30% pray weekly. It grows from there. People in their 60s pray even more—75% say they pray daily—and another 15% pray weekly.

PEOPLE PRAY DAILY

How do we pray the best? We tend to break with what we're doing and close our eyes, or stop all our talk and fall silent a moment. But God is not only in silence but right in the noise and the voices and the wind and the excitement. God is not only in the darkness of closed eyes but in the color and confusion and discoveries and excitement of wide open eyes. In a word, we are always in God's presence.

Still we feel right—and we are right—in falling silent and in closing eyes if it helps—because our God is an Otherness. That is the first thing we know about God: God is very much unlike ourselves. Some spiritualities would even say God is not really personal. Why use words to speak to One who, in one sense, has no hearing? Because, whatever God may be, WE need the words. Whatever words we use in prayer are, like the tight-rope walker's fans, just there to keep us centered. We cannot really imagine God at all—for God has no form, no shape, no size, no dimensions, no color, nothing that is imaginable.

GOD IS UNIMAGINABLE

Unimaginable God, Holy Mystery, how shall we pray?

We can only *be* in God's presence, and do so consciously, knowingly—and that can be the fullness of prayer. Existing, alert to God's presence, alert to our links to others: that is the best prayer.

IN GOD'S PRESENCE

That is what I mean by centering.

Still, prayer is not the best word to describe this, since the word "prayer" implies begging. "I pray, sir, a penny." That's a "prayer." Synonyms are invocation, petition, plea, and request. That's not really what we're talking about here.

The difficulty: if you know how love feels, and if you believe that God is a loving parent, a loving companion, a loving Love, then one can understand how it's almost an insult to beg from God—since, if divine love is infinite, we must already have everything God can give us. But haven't we heard that God wants us to pray, to beg? Yes, we've heard that, but it can't be true, not for those who know and realize that God is Love. Still, the impulse to speak to God, to be consciously in God's presence, is found in all religions and religious instincts. Might there be a better word for it than prayer?

There must be—but what is it? Contemplation? Too opaque. Meditation? Too cerebral. Worship? Too limiting. Reflection? Incomplete. Awe? Reverence? Listening? None of them do it. Perhaps, like the God we pray to, communication with God—or better, communication *toward* God—is unnameable.

GOD IS AND WE ARE So we return to where we started: we can be in God's presence, consciously. We can be centered. Nothing we see or hear, and not silence or darkness either, is God. But God IS, a vibrant ocean of livingness, creativity, and relationship. And we ARE. Two presences are we, unequal but still face to face, or, better, interwoven and inter-existing, a little like a child in a mother's womb, or an infant in a father's hug, or a limited spirit with an infinite and unlimited spirit, and wind within a wind, invisible and noiseless: that begins to describe prayer, adult prayer.

So, how shall we go about raising our heart and mind to God, the action we've always called "prayer?" My own answer is: each in our own bewildered way. Whatever feels comfortable, that's good-enough prayer. The more centered we are, the more balanced and expansive will be the result.

PRAYER WITHOUT WORDS One other suggestion: God speaks all around and within us, but not in words, rather in everything that is created. So, as God does not speak in words, we may choose to reply the same way, not in words, but just in what we are.

4

Perhaps then we can define prayer as "being what we are—consciously—before God, and waiting...." Words help us enter. Waiting for God: not a bad word for what we now call prayer. Not a bad word for life itself. Or an enlightened life. Waiting for the appearance of God on stage, waiting for a visit from God, waiting for God to arrive. Waiting for the future: which is always God: the Divine—inhabiting everything that really is, all the way to the horizon, and that horizon ever receding.

ABOUT THESE PRAYERS

There are several elements in each of these thirty prayer experiences. First there is *Mindfulness,* which I think of as Step One in coming to Centering: it is simply a word for becoming reflective and self-aware. The *Centering Reflections* themselves are next. Then *Words of Jesus* and words *From Another Faith,* both of which offer unique insights about the theme. These are followed by a *Meditation, Praying with a Psalm,* a *Practice for Today,* and finally a *Mantra* or prayer refrain to keep the centering experience fresh throughout the day. Usually there is a bug or "critter" prayer at the end of the experience to "lighten your heart."

While written primarily for individuals, *In God's Presence* may be also useful for community prayer. It is for both "Circles and Solitudes." Group members can take turns reading various sections, and everyone in the group can pray the psalms together. Pauses for response or for silent reflection can be inserted to meet the needs of the group.

RICH RESOURCES

Three books, aside from the bible, have been indispensable resources for me: *She Who Is* by Elizabeth Johnson (Crossroad, New York, 1993), a brilliant fresh elucidation of the problems of discourse about God; and the two collections: *Earth Prayers,* edited by Elizabeth Roberts and Elias Amidon (HarperSanFrancisco, 1991), and *The Oxford Book of Prayer,* edited by George Appleton (Oxford University Press, New York, 1985).

In my text, direct quotations are acknowledged. Many paraphrases of prayers I found in translation are my own, as are the words from the bible.

My hope in what follows is for both usefulness and "orthopraxis": usefulness in finding rich meaning beneath life's greatest mysteries; and orthopraxis (or "correct action") flowing from a constant concern for the oppressed and needy in solidarity with the Divine Wisdom of God manifest in Jesus of Nazareth.

May we often find ourselves where the oppressed are, and may we bring them often into our own center.

William Cleary
Shelburne, Vermont

1

God of Fire

See me here, look to you, my God.
You are part of my every move;
How rich a day it can be!

MINDFULNESS

Creating God, Fire at the heart of everything,
Three-fold Communion of Wisdom,
Care, and Creativity,
I know not how to pray.
I listen and hear only silence,
I look but you are invisible.
Silent, Invisible Fire,
Give me spiritual eyes, believing eyes, to in-see with,
Give me the hearing to catch
every thinnest hint of your music,
those undeniable harmonies, those subtle rhythms.

CENTERING

Burning Fire at the heart of everything—
every greening sprig of grass,
every up-beat song swallow,
even of the milky moon
that watches over the sunrise—
burn inside me as well.

Teach me to pray,
Breath Within, Spirit-Wind Within,
give me burning words of prayer, born of your Fire.
Let me warm in the heat of patient centering,
Let me burst into orange and yellow tongues
that speak worship.

Burning Fire of Justice,
give me a vision of your irresistible desires:
to set things right that are grotesquely wrong,
to let everything that is good grow as it wants to,
to satisfy every hunger,
end every loneliness,
mend every heartbreak,
and to entrust every unavoidable evil
to the healing mystery of your infinite meaning.

WORDS OF JESUS I came to bring fire to the earth and how I wish it were already kindled! I have a cleansing with which to be cleansed, and what stress I am under until it is completed!

—Luke 12:49

FROM ANOTHER FAITH O Thou who are the God of all names
And the Maker of the Heavens,
I beseech you
To make of my prayer a fire
that will burn away the veils
which have shut me out from thy beauty,
and a light that will lead me
to the ocean of thy presence.

—Baha'i daily prayer

MEDITATION People often pray facing east, facing the fire. That's where the sun rises, the great traditional, masculine God-symbol: God, high and glorious in his far-away isolation, warm with splendor and love, power and mystery, giving the feeling of warmth and newness coming toward us from him, the Lord. The sun in the east symbolizes it all. Prayerful people almost naturally face the warm sun in facing the divine.

But now consider praying facing west, toward good Mother Earth—a different God-symbol—as she rolls toward us and toward the sun: Mother Earth sporting her lakes and haphazard mountains, heavy with her homeless and innocent children, scarred with inner cities and polluting industries, alive with tens of thousands of lovers celebrating love in their beds and wheelchairs, with humans tilling her fertile surface with loving seed-full hands, reaping her wonderful flavors and medicinal plants, rich with animals enormous or tiny, domesticated or wild, familiar or exotic: all wonderfully mysterious: Mother Earth with her center and heart aflame, with her face full of age-marked beauty, her body still rich with fertility, with her cities full of ecstasy and agony.

Spinning along, creating our days and nights, she carries us on her back around the sun, herself a daughter of the original fireball that burst across the cosmos at the beginning of time.

Sometimes try to pray facing west, addressing an ever more mystifying, more connected-to-us Divinity.

Happy are they whose help is in God,
The God of Jacob and Rachel,
Who hope in the Spirit, their God and their All,
The maker of earth and of heaven.

Come, Holy Fire
Of life and desire.

You called the depths of the sea into being,
And all of the creatures within it,
A God who keeps faith and who saves the oppressed,
And gives nourishing food to the hungry.

Come, Holy Fire
Of life and desire.

Our God is the one who sets prisoners free
And opens the eyes of the blind.
Who raises the heads of those that were crushed,
And loves the workers of justice.

Come, Holy Fire
Of life and desire.

God guards every step of the sojourner's path,

And protects the orphan and widow.
Our God shall win over the forces of wrong
And reign triumphant forever.

Come, Holy Fire
Of life and desire.

God of fire, in community with those I love, connecting with them at least in my spirit, may I find genuine enthusiasm today for the work you lay before me. Share with me your wisdom, care, and creativity. Set me on fire.

Come, Holy Fire
Of life and desire.

TO LIGHTEN YOUR HEART

THE FEARFUL FIREFLY

Creator of both night and day,
I do not understand your way,
The other fireflies and I,
   see many things that mystify.

Oh, yes, we're glad to be alive,
And through the years we've learned to thrive.
It's fun from darkest night till dawn
To flash and twinkle on the lawn.

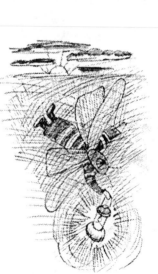

But we are terrified of day
When we must put our lamps away
And close our eyes and cease our fun
Till nightfall drives away the sun.
What kind of horrid creatures play in daylight?
Can they see their way?

O God of Every Mystery, give us clear eyes so we can see
How any world of wonder must
Have room for other things than us,
Strange things that love the frightening day!
And while we're sleeping,
   wake and play!

2

Holy Wisdom, My God

I'll think of today as a New Day.
My feelings may be a bit novel
since I have a new name even for God,
or at least an old name with a new ring to it.

MINDFULNESS

Holy Wisdom, my God,
Sophia as you are named in the Greek translations
of the Book of Wisdom,
Divine Spirit,
in whom we live and move and have our being,
like womb-dwellers we rejoice in your surrounding care.

CENTERING

In embryonic darkness we reach out to you
trying to understand you at least a little.
Ever-existing, inexhaustible Source of all that is,
I rest in my dim inkling of who you are.
It comforts me to know you are there, are here,
and are Wisdom.

Supreme Being giving us being,
Supreme Wisdom giving us wisdom,
reaching out with definitive self-expression in our Messiah,
incarnate in love wherever love thrives,

energizing us all in your inexhaustibly wise Spirit
that, like the wind, comes and goes unseen.
I praise you, Giver of life and mystery,
pervading the cosmos like a mother bird
hovering over the primordial chaos,
sheltering those in trouble
under the protective shadow of your care,
bearing up the enslaved on your great wings
toward freedom and shalom.

Like a quietly ever-present midwife,
you work with those in pain
to bring about an ever-new creation.
Like an all-patient washerwoman you scrub away all stains
till we are like new,
then you hide, pretending not to be,
almost out of reach of our gratitude.
World-mothering Spirit,
Unimaginably Creative Ocean of Being,
I rest in your presence and caring vitality.

WORDS
OF JESUS How often have I longed to gather your children, as a
mother hen gathers her chicks under her wings, but you
were not willing, and so you are left empty and desolate....   —*Matthew 23:37*

FROM
ANOTHER
FAITH O God, enemy of folly and ignorance,
grant me the joy that all beings may see me
with the eye of a friend,
and that I see all beings
with the eye of a friend,
and that all beings see all beings
with the eye of a friend.
                                        —*Vedic Prayer*

MEDITATION The only way we know anything about God is in looking
at creatures we admire. We call God "Father" because we
admire fathers. We may call God "Mother" for the same
reason. Of late we have as a society undergone a change
with regard to women. From second-class citizenship
women have risen in the minds of many to equality in

12

every important respect, and even ascendancy in crucial areas. Women's amazing ability to bear and bring forth human life, to make fast friends, and to live much longer than men despite all their long hours of work, has made observant males envious.

Applying these admirable qualities to God almost creates a new God for us. Today we hear new names for God also—feminine names like Sister, Nurse, Sophia—as writers and speakers work with the new interest in the feminine qualities in God. For many reasons feminine names for God are helpful.

They express the exuberance of love in God and the power of that love to keep empowering-to-exist whatever there is of beauty, liveliness, and promise in creation, standing strongly in opposition to the forces of evil and non-being, violence and hatred.

Using feminine names for God also promotes the flourishing of women and therefore of all creation since, if loss of a species, however tiny, is intuited to be tragic in the interlaced ecosystem we all live in, oppression of half the entire human race is unmistakably supremely tragic; and therefore its flourishing instead of being suppressed surely benefits everyone on earth greatly.

W̲ho is like God, our God,
Who is seated in the heavens,
Who looks far down upon the skies and the earth
Who fills the earth with justice?

I join my voice to all creation's praise,
Knowing that you surround us all our days.

God raises the poor from the dust,
And lifts the needy from the ash heap,
To make them sit with princes,
With the very princes of Earth.
God gives the barren woman a home,
Making her the joyous mother of children.

I join my voice to all creation's praise,
Knowing that you surround us all our days.

Bless God, O servants of God.
Blessed be the power of God's own name
From this time forth and for evermore.
From the rising of the sun to its setting
The name of God be praised!

I join my voice to all creation's praise,
Knowing that you surround us all our days.

God of Wisdom, make me wise enough today to put no limitations on you, for then my greatest expectations will not be disappointed in the long run. Show me how to rest in your presence and caring vitality, and to see all beings with the eyes of a mother and friend.

I join my voice to all creation's praise, Knowing that you surround us all our days.

TO LIGHTEN YOUR HEART

THE LADYBUG'S LAMENT

Forgive me, God, for crying out, you're not the one to blame,
You know the curse that saddens me, the burden of my name.
Yes, I was born a "Ladybug," but of the male persuasion,
My world is all female defined,
    no matter the occasion!

They own the church, they run the world, they credit or condemn,
They make a mess, then ask us males to clean it up for them.
They think of You as female too! Believe me, that's the worst.
A female God makes males a joke,
    invisible and cursed.

Dear God, give them new eyes to see how you gave double powers
To solve the puzzles of the world and make creation ours.
The sexes are not opposite, but different, not the same,
Males bring new genius,
    and new strength and not just a new name.

Sexism is a brutal sin and leaves us males accurs'd,
How would the ladies like it if our roles were reversed?
They'd curse like fiends and then explode like nitroglycerin,
So let them sweat it not if we get strident now and then.

14

3

I Do Not
Stand Alone

I turn to you in prayer:
myself with all my relationships,
all my memories, all my potentialities,
all my embodied self.

I do not stand alone before you, unknown God,
here in the darkness of my solitude.
I have ties of relationship
to the whole web of life and being
around and under me, behind me and in front of me.
Aloneness is an illusion.

I am bound in love to my immediate family.
Their concerns, their fears,
their hopes, their joys are mine too.
But mine also must be the sorrows
of those trapped in low paying jobs,
those of an oppressed minority, afraid of their neighbors,
those who live in dread of illness or injury,
or who lack health security,
and those who feel friendless, despondent,

MINDFULNESS

CENTERING

discouraged, or desperate:
the human family all over the world with all its sorrows.
See me as one with them all,
lead me to that expansion of heart,
Communioning Spirit.

But before you I stand with ties to the joyful also,
to the hopeful, to the thriving,
to lovers young and old,
to builders, inventors, creators,
designers, and discoverers,
to those jogging, dancing, climbing,
rolling happily down highways, flying.
They are all my human family,
and I am tied to them in their human glories.

I do not stand here alone;
I am Earth's child as well,
a small part of her mysteriously thriving life,
breathing her atmosphere,
living from her fruits and vegetables,
a companion of all her animals,
with ties of reverence
to all her amazing continents and oceans,
to the mysteries of her mammoth body beneath me
and of her role as a planet in the cosmos.
In your eyes I stand before you
linked into the whole web of being around me.
May it be so in my eyes as well.

WORDS OF JESUS If you are offering your gift at the altar, and there
remember that your brother has something against you,
leave your gift there before the altar and go and first be
reconciled to your brother, and then come and
offer your gift.   —*Matthew 5:23–24*

FROM ANOTHER FAITH I bow to thee, O God of the sandbanks
and in the midst of the current as well.
I bow to thee, God of the little pebbles
and in the serene stretches of the waters.
I bow to thee, God suffusing everything,

in uninhabited desert,
and in the crowded homes.
I bow to thee.
   —*Vedic Prayer, First Century*

Theologian Elizabeth Johnson states that relationship is "the fundamental code of the world." Why code, a kind of secret language that must be known before we can read a message? And why call it fundamental, as if relationship and relationships with others stand first in our lives?

Perhaps the theologian means that while there is for Judeo-Christians but one God, the God of Isaac, Jacob, and Jesus, that God is not solitary. In the Hebrew Scriptures the one God Yahweh ("I Am") has many kinds of presences and names, appearing as Creating Wisdom, as the Accompanying Shekinah, as the awesome Whirlwind, as King, as Savior from slavery, as Father in Heaven. In the Christian Scriptures these names are endorsed, and added are God as Brother and Messiah, as Pregnant Mother (in whom we live and move and have our being), as Liberator (pushing princes from their thrones and raising up the lowly).

In every case, our single God has multiple relationships within the divinity, most clearly distinguished in the late-arriving image of a Holy Trinity: a creating Father, a co-creating and earth-visiting Son, and a Holy Spirit swirling between them and coming upon believers like fire. Theologian Johnson stretches this image in another direction when she renames the Trinity: 1) Spirit–Sophia, pervading the world with vitalizing and liberating power; 2) Jesus–Sophia, embodying the compassionate love of heaven for earth; 3) Holy Wisdom, the unoriginate Mother of all things, upholding the world.

So ours is a God with inner relationships of some kind, and whom we do not know except as in relationship with us: our creating, liberating, enlightening, God—a Holy Communion of Inexhaustible Vitality that creates us. Not only that: we creatures find ourselves unable to begin or carry on our life without numerous relationships with other humans and with all other creatures. So the essential relatedness within our God is stamped on ourselves as well. Relatedness, friendship, communion is an essential of our lives—and in fact the concept of relatedness and relationship is "the fundamental code of the world."

Our dealing with what is mysterious and unintelligible around us depends on our grasping the code within all creation: relationship. From top to bottom, our life consists of relationships. To think that at any time we "stand alone" is an illusion. To value complete non-dependence, separation, and aloofness—any kind of classism—is a mistake that inevitably impoverishes our lives.

PRAYING WITH PSALM 36

O God, your love is limitless as sky,
Your faithfulness lives high above the clouds,
Your justice firm as awesome mountain peaks,
Your judgments deep as any ocean's floor.

We reach toward you a hundred times a day
And know that you are there and hear us pray.

How precious is your strong and steady love,
The human family thrives beneath your wings,
We feast on the abundance of your grace,
And taste each day refreshment in your house.

We reach toward you a hundred times a day
And know that you are there and hear us pray.

You are the source of all the streams of life,
And it is in your light that we see light,
We all rejoice to have your steadfast love
To rescue us from anguish and despair.

We reach toward you a hundred times a day
And know that you are there and hear us pray.

PRACTICE FOR TODAY

May I be blest enough today to recognize that I am in solidarity with the whole human race, for then I will be walking in the light of reality.

MANTRA

We reach toward you a hundred times a day
And know that you are there and hear us pray. ❑

4

Lover of Clowns

I can stand on my head, looking at your feet.
I can make a frightening face, my God,
stopping you in your tracks.
More amazing: I can stand on my feet,
and jump and run.
I can smile. I can pray.

MINDFULNESS

Comedian God with an audience afraid to laugh
(as Voltaire said),
how much oddness there is in your world!
We know of some:
atoms that contain, in infinitismal space,
mammoth earth-shaking forces,
insects that resemble the twigs they live among,
lizards that change their color at will,
spiders that lure a moth by mimicking its scent,
stinkbugs, skunks, stinkfish,
that disgust their enemies to defeat them.

CENTERING

What an inexhaustably queer place is this planet.

Some vastly whimsical inventor is at work.
One almost has to be a clown to fit in.

Did the same Love that made skunks make me?
Did the same Mind that set the speed of light
concoct my unique DNA?
Mysterious Creator,
Incomparable Genius of Loving Wit,
How clownish our attempts to relate to you.

I will try to keep them clownish.
That seems to be a style you enjoy the most.

WORDS OF JESUS

I thank you, God of heaven and earth, that you have hidden these things from the wise and understanding, and revealed them to little ones.

—Luke 10:21

FROM ANOTHER FAITH

In your image let me pattern my life, O God.
Let me awake with your name on my lips.
In my eyes let me ever carry your image
so I may perceive you—and you alone—
in every one I meet.

—Zoroaster, Sixth Century BCE

MEDITATION

Why are clowns so fascinating?
The oversize mouth, the elephant ears,
the giant lens-less glasses,
the bulbous nose, the tattered formal clothes,
the laughable shoes, the tears over nonsense,
the pretensions to grandeur,
the pratfalls, the dangling broken watch,
the empty suitcase hanging open:
everyone loves a clown.
    That's me at times:
psychotic about trifles,
unable to cope with being ordinary,
under the illusion that I am unloved and lost,
then the next moment living the delusion
that I am one of the immortals,
upset by my stumbling walk,

my insufficient talent,
my oversize ego, my humorous desires,
my bogus heroism,
unacceptant of my inheritance:
an amazing body-mind self,
a rich experience, an everlasting promise.
What a clown!
Entertaining, I hope.
Beloved? Well, sure.

I reverence you, my God, my only strength,
The Most High is my rock, my fort, my safety,
My God, a perfect tower where I rest,
My shield, my source of joy, my firm stronghold.

Hear me, Great Spirit, loving, giving, freeing,
In You I live and move and have my being.

The enemy came on to bring me sorrow,
But God became my harbor and my rest
And brought me forth into a broader pasture
And saved me, since I was God's great delight.

Hear me, Great Spirit, loving, giving, freeing,
In You I live and move and have my being.

The Holy One has loved me for my faith,
And I delight in you, my Spirit God,
You light my lamp, illuminate my darkness,
You give me safety from my every fear.

Hear me, Great Spirit, loving, giving, freeing,
In You I live and move and have my being.

God is Shield for all who offer thanks,
For who is god besides the God we know?
And who can grant us safety but our God,
The one who girded us with strength within?

Hear me, Great Spirit, loving, giving, freeing,
In You I live and move and have my being.

God made my feet like those of swiftest deer,
And set me safely on the greatest heights.
There I shall stay and sing in constant praise

And live safe in the shadow of my God.

Hear me, Great Spirit, loving, giving, freeing,
In You I live and move and have my being.

PRACTICE
FOR
TODAY God, Lover of Clowns, show me
how to take myself lightly today,
that I might soar.
Remind me often that the same Love
that made monkeys made me.
Teach me to love much today
and to laugh often.

MANTRA Hear me, Great Spirit, loving, giving, freeing,
In You I live and move and have my being.

TO LIGHTEN YOUR HEART

A MONKEY'S MEDITATION

O God, most tolerant of foolishness,
I scratch my head: am I a favorite son?
Although my face looks ancient as the hills
And I devour bananas by the ton?

I can't be serious— you have not made me so.
You'll have to love me as I am: a clown,
Swinging along and screeching like a fool,
And sometimes praying hanging upside-down.

Am I your favorite? Look, I'll make a face,
Hang by my tail, yawn like a crocodile,
Seek out your fleas, dear God, if you have some—
It is enough if I but make you smile.

Deep in my heart there is one serious place
where I retreat for hurricanes at night,
clinging to you with all my clownish strength,
hoping the One I cling to's holding tight.

5

When Hope
Is Gone

Who but you will ever know my heart's sorrow?
When hope is gone,
through all the darkness and suffocation,
I wonder: is there a breeze of meaning anywhere?
Are you there?

MINDFULNESS

When hope is gone, and all is lost,
and the earth crumbles beneath my feet,
set me down in a new heaven and a new earth,
God of everlasting creativity,
divine inventor of every kind of life,
Fathomless Ocean of Energy and Love.

CENTERING

When I disappoint myself with lack of success,
a shrunken imagination,
the limitations of my heart,
come upon me
with the scented breeze of your new possibilities,
persistent Encourager.

When doors close me in,
when windows are opaque,

and I beat against destiny,
to let me enter what I dream of,
lead me by the hand
to where your darkness turns to dawn.

When I am parched with fever and defeat,
and there is no more strength
for the struggle that is going so badly,
give me streams of living water
springing up within my own soul,
you who gave such steadfast faith to our ancestors.

WORDS
OF JESUS

God is with me and also with you.
I am telling you this because
I want you to experience my peace.
In the world you will have trouble, but be brave:
I have overcome the world.

—*John 16:33*

FROM
ANOTHER
FAITH

Of that which we dread,
Healer God, make us fearless.
O Generous One, assist us with your help.
May the air we breathe sweep fearlessness into us:
fearlessness on earth,
fearlessness in the heavens.
May fearlessness be our guard in front and behind us.
May fearlessness encompass us above and below.
May we lose all fear of friend or enemy.
May we not fear the known or the unknown.
May we not fear the night or the day.
This day may all the world be our friend.

—*Vedic Prayer*

MEDITATION

My heart breaks
When I have to part with dreams
That put me where I thought that I should be,
When hopes that grew within my dearest schemes
Died in my hands, a crushing tragedy.

I'll sweep up all the chips left on the floor,
A brief obituary and a wake,

A burial, then I shall mourn no more.
(But wait! Could there not have been a mistake?)

Fear and despair are companions. If we can only think positively, half the struggle is won. Prayer is usually one positive thing that we can reach to whenever we're surrounded by feelings of negativity.

Steven Biko told his crushed and nearly hopeless followers: "Begin to think of yourselves as human beings." That might be a starting point for someone in despair over the condition of the oppressed, or the crushing events of one's life. "I am a human being. I am a member of this family of humanity. I have a role. I am part of it. Crushed, pushed out, defeated as I feel, I am not alone. I am a human, one of so many. I endure each defeat in solidarity with all."

And we are in solidarity with God as well, if we accept the thought of the martyr and theologian Dietrich Bonhoeffer. Instead of going to God in search of help, he says we rather "go to God when he is sore bestead, find him poor and scorned, without shelter or bread, whelmed with the weight of the wicked, weak, and dead."

PRAYING WITH PSALM 6

Be gracious to me, O God, I am your child,
Heal the despair you hear in my Amen,
For you can take the turmoil from my soul
And give me total peace within again.

You know, dear God, my present and my past,
I trust in you as long as life shall last.

How long before you shall deliver me?
How long before you come to save my life?
Because of your great love, I trust in you
Despite the doubts that give me inner strife.

You know, dear God, my present and my past,
I trust in you as long as life shall last.

PRACTICE FOR TODAY

God of Everlasting Creativity,
fill me with streams of your living water today
and give me hope and a steadfast faith.

Remind me that I have been given your peace
and thus there are no limitations.
Persistent Encourager, give me today
the scented breeze of your new possibilities.

MANTRA   You know, dear God, my present and my past,
I trust in you as long as life shall last.

ASPIRATIONS OF AN ANT

I haven't time to pray, there's work to do today.
My ant brigade is underpaid
And rushed in every way.

I'm just a nervous wreck,
With pains in back and neck.
Call me a creep, this ant hole's deep
And I'm no architect.

So labor is my prayer,
And mostly it's despair.
My friends and I dig, haul, and sigh,
And swear that life's unfair.

Dear God, forgive our tears,
Our grumblings and our fears.
Come, do your will in our ant hill,
Until our Christ appears.

He'll crawl among us then, an anthill citizen.
And teach us ways to give you praise
Despite our plight. Amen.

6

In Peace of Soul

Mysterious God of earth and sky,
woods and stream, air and ocean,
each day almost a million *kinds* of animals
look to you—as I do.
You are our life.

MINDFULNESS

Mysterious Divine Presence, God of Peace,
living here with me today in everything that is,
so—in my heart and mind and stomach and hands—
I begin my prayer in peace of soul.

CENTERING

My day's task is not impossible,
rather it is natural,
and harmonious with you
and with everything around me:
harmonious with death,
and every one of life's disappointments,
accidents, and mistakes;
harmonious in some sense even with every birth
and spurt of growth
and enlargement of mind
and creative achievement all around me as well.

My day's task is to "go with" all this music,
to fit in,
to carry out my melodious task
to the full extent of my ability—
but no more than that: a manageable role.
I know I am not called to be other than I am
or to do more than I can.
And while I will sigh with the mourners of death,
I will also dance with the drummers of life,
believing there is a music in it all,
had we ears to hear.

WORDS OF JESUS

Go learn what this means: I have desired mercy
not sacrifices. Then you will know that I have come to
call sinners, not the righteous.

—*Matthew 9:13*

FROM ANOTHER FAITH

Cover my eyes from the sight of evil,
Close my ears from the sound of useless words,
Protect my heart from unfaithful thoughts,
And my veins from the hint of transgression.
Guide these feet to the paths of your desires,
And your faultless ways,
And may your compassion be turned toward me.

—*Prayer from the Jewish Berakoth*

MEDITATION

Wouldn't the children of God be more at peace if they learned to say "please" less and "thank you" more? Does a parent like to hear a fervent importunate "please" or "have mercy" when one is already doing infinitely more than the child could dream or ask, and is already feeling limitless sympathy?

Our patient divine parent accepts our every prayer, however halting; but the better prayer is to trust that mercy is there for us, despite any appearance to the contrary. There is just no way to pinch God.

All our extraordinary efforts to get God's attention would be better spent expanding our minds or comforting the afflicted. There is no way to manipulate God or the future: by reciting set prayers, for instance, that are supposed to be powerful or effective, by burnt sacrifices or gratuitous pain endured. It is the ordinary humane life that "works." Not sacrifices but mercy is what true religion is about.

PRAYING
WITH
PSALM 4

Dear God, I am before your face today,
You warm me with the comfort of your gaze,
For you have put a joy within my heart
More true than would a gift of wealth or praise.

My worrying can cease,
Your presence is my peace.

In silence I retire within my heart
And quiet fires of deep communion start.
In peace I lay me down at night and sleep
For you alone, Great Spirit, my soul keep.

My worrying can cease,
Your presence is my peace.

Dear God, I am before your face this hour,
You comfort me with knowledge of your ways,
For you have put a joy within my heart
More true than any gift of wealth or praise.

My worrying can cease,
Your presence is my peace.

PRACTICE
FOR
TODAY

Mysterious God of earth and sky,
give me peace of soul today
and show me how to offer mercy to all
and judgment to none.
Above all help me to see that the circle
of those I love is a true incarnation of your presence.

MANTRA

My worrying can cease,
Your presence is my peace.

AN INCHWORM'S ALLELUIA

Dear God, is any bug more calculating
Than are we inchworms, shyly tiptoeing,
Measuring our steps, so we will know the number
Of thanks we owe for your empowering?

We may not move as fast as others do,
But we get joy from dancing in a loop,
Omega-shaped, then stretched out toward the future,
Then with feet hunched again, we forward swoop.

Happy, we thrive, yet as we thrive we change!
Alas, we'll soon turn into moths who fly
Uncalculated distances aloft,
Infinite inches, up into the sky.

On that bright day, O God, may we remember
Each journey always with one small step starts,
And trust that, though you once gave us but inches,
You've dreams for us far greater than our hearts.

7

I Cannot Pray

As simply as flowers turn toward the sun
for their warmth and excitement,
or lovers turn toward the moon,
feeling filled with mystery,
so, out of great need and great awe,
I raise my heart and mind to you,
Exuberant Communioning Aliveness,
My God.

MINDFULNESS

My prayer will be my distractions today,
dear God, elusive mystery,
for I have nothing else to offer you.
That does not surprise you, of course,
though it is not a welcome phenomenon for me.
I desire to pray,
I want to enjoy your presence
but I cannot.
I am besieged with other thoughts and feelings.

CENTERING

You see, I am the way you have made me:
a jumble of energies, muscles, glands, memories—

and this is what I bring before your eyes:
this chaos that is my inner self.
I am, science says, a torrent of micro-events,
violently busy atoms, cells, organs,
all working—astonishingly—as one:
more like a rushing river than anything solid.

The only prayer I can make
is to remain present here.
You will have to read my vibes,
my surging currents, my rock-tossed spray.
I desire to be before you, to look toward you,
to see my role in life with a little wisdom,
to offer myself to life as it will come.
And if I am, despite my feelings,
still a splendid creation,
then I give glory to you
despite my limitations,
my distracted mind, my chaotic imagination,
my wayward heart.

WORDS OF JESUS

In praying, do not heap up empty phrases
like the pagans do.
They think that they will be heard
because they use so many words.
Do not be like them, for God knows what you need
before you even ask.

—Matthew 6:7–8

FROM ANOTHER FAITH

I speak with reverence before the great Parent God:
I pray that, as a child of God,
I may not be taken hold of by narrow desires
but show forth the divine glory
by living a life of wide creativity—
growing from an authentic self.

—Shinto Prayer

MEDITATION

We carry on with prayer even when it seems to get us nowhere: but be creative. Do not keep doing what seems pointless and boring. Solitude is not always the best situation for prayer, but it can be a start. In solitude we can center ourselves, name our strengths and weaknesses, and prepare for the next encounter with day-to-day reality.

But remember that our prayers and dedication are not going to increase God's compassion, or move the Creator to do something that would otherwise not have happened. We are already the objects of God's "infinite" care, and even theoretically nothing can be added to "infinite." Still, to turn to God in prayer is instinctual, and to do so somehow connected to others, at least in spirit, is ideal.

There is an important sense in which prayers said with words are useless—because God reads our actions. We do form words, and the words express our desires and help us think straight. Most importantly, the *act* of praying is what God receives, along with all the other actions of our lives. Those are the real words we say: actions expressing right judgment, mercy, faith: feeding the hungry, visiting the sick, caring for the poor and desperate, remembering the forgotten, caring for the planet, creating beauty, reverencing wonders, bearing wrongs patiently, listening. These are the prayers God cannot but hear and answer.

The heavens are telling the glory of God
And the sky shows forth God's handiwork.
Day unto day pours forth good news,
And night unto night shows starry beauty.

PRAYING
WITH
PSALM 19

Great God, to whom all mysteries belong,
I add my whisper to your cosmic song.

Though wordless and speechless are heavenly lights,
Yet their voices go out through all the earth,
Their words stretch to the edge of the world
And echo throughout the universe.

Great God, to whom all mysteries belong,
I add my whisper to your cosmic song.

In the heavens God has set up a tent for the sun,
Who strides forth like a bridegroom at the dawn,
Like an athlete he runs a daily course.
Rising from the end of the heavens,
His track circles on to the other horizon,

and nothing can hide from his heat.

Great God, to whom all mysteries belong,
I add my whisper to your cosmic song.

God, elusive mystery,
within your strengthening presence today,
help me to launch out once again
in my search for meaning,
undismayed by the absurdity that surrounds me.
I place my wayward heart in your hands.
Guide me that I might at every moment
raise my heart and mind to you.

Great God, to whom all mysteries belong,
I add my whisper to your cosmic song.

TO LIGHTEN YOUR HEART

A TROUBLED TOAD'S REFLECTION

I wail!—Good God, you've made me but a toad,
Wrong size, wrong skin, wrong color, wrong abode!
I rarely jump no matter how you goad.
I'm slow and weak and fat and pigeon-toed.

But wait, here comes my lovely toady bride!
She loves me! How I blush and try to hide!
She cherishes my smile, demure and wide,
And loves my throaty croak at eventide!

Look down upon your miracle of life,
Dear God, a toad unsung by drum and fife,
But grateful for my place, and free of strife—
(especially in the hot tub with my wife).

34

8

You Are Home

O Mystery all around me and within me,
the journey gets long
when we have no respite.
I'll stop here and rest
and put myself together
in the presence of your Holy Mystery.

MINDFULNESS

Closer than my skin,
closer than my eyes,
closer than my thought is to my self,
here you are, Unimaginable God.
From you I emerge at each split second,
toward you I move, moment by moment,
to you I inexorably go: you are home.

CENTERING

So I am not homeless in life—
though I am wandering,
unsure of tomorrow's place.
But I have a home toward which I am drawn hour by hour:
It is you.
For this world *is* unified, is a creation that fits together,
and you are its magnetic center,
all of us together are drawn to you,

toward Shalom, toward home.
And even now we find you within ourselves,
at home there.

We call our journey's end heaven,
but that is an image convenient
to the limitations of our imagination,
the blue, welcoming, unapproachable sky, "the heavens."
The reality is beyond our imagining
though we know it is there.
And it is you, God of my heart,
closer than my skin,
closer than my eyes,
closer than my thought is to my self,
here you are, Unimaginable God.

WORDS OF JESUS Those who love me will keep my word,
and my father will love them,
and we shall come to them
and make our home with them.

—John 14:23

FROM ANOTHER FAITH Let me not wander in vain.
Let me not work in vain.
Let me not make my home with the narrow-minded.
Let me not lose the company of the enlightened.
Let me not lose my tempered self.
Let me not stray from the road of goodness.
Let me not over-strive, either for this day
or for tomorrow,
This is the wealth I ask of you, God of Endless Possibility.

—Pattinatar, Tenth Century

MEDITATION Sometimes we reach toward God in wordless prayer—
but is anything happening? One way to understand it is to
consider that the cosmos around us is full of flying objects—whirling, orbiting, somersaulting, streaking, drift-
ing, and shooting objects—but some are on fire and some
are not. Those that are on fire are called stars.

About six billion human beings inhabit our earth. All
are wrapped in the mystery of God, but not all are hunt-

ing for God in the dark corners of creation, alert to intimations of the transcendent, asking ultimate questions. Not all are on fire with the search for God which is prayer.

Prayer is a kind of starfire.

And such starfire burns in many humans. In a way it burns, at least smolderingly, in us all. What adult does not, at least occasionally, ask the question Why? Who does not feel thankful for occasional luck, even when we have no human helper to give the thanks to or no human companion to tell about our delight? Who is not sometimes in awe of sun, moon, blue sky, and green earth, deer, dragonflies, hummingbirds, elephants? Or find themselves marveling at human beauty, astounding courage, or the charism for inventiveness in the people around us? What is there but awe in our hearts to hear of the earth's origins, of the near-unbelievable dimensions of our cosmos, of the wonders of the earth's self-regulating qualities, of the phenomena of evolution?

Those feelings are the sparks of starfire, of prayer, and words do not begin to express them. "Unspeakable groanings" was the description given by Paul of Tarsus. Often such prayer happens silently. Seldom is it logical or orderly. It is more than a little like catching fire, or, better, bursting quietly into flame. But it may light up the heavens, for all we know, like starfire, streaking, whirling, somersaulting through space.

Dear God, you have been home to us
since long before even the mountains were born,
long before you formed the earth,
you are God.

You are the home we're made for, Loving Friend,
And restless are we till our journey's end.

Teach us so to number our days,
that we may have a heart of wisdom.
For behold, you can but say a word
and we return to dust: and so we are gone.

You are the home we're made for, Loving Friend,

PRAYING
WITH
PSALM 90

And restless are we till our journey's end.

For in your eyes, a thousand earthly years pass
as did yesterday, or as one watch of the night.
In each life's evening we are swept away like grass.
By morning everything is new.

You are the home we're made for, Loving Friend,
And restless are we till our journey's end.

PRACTICE
FOR
TODAY Unimaginable God, remind me today
that I am with you and always at home in you.
I am never homeless.
May I freely welcome others into my home this day.

MANTRA You are the home we're made for, Loving Friend,
And restless are we till our journey's end.

TO LIGHTEN YOUR HEART

THE MATINS OF A SLUG

I move in you, Creative God, then rest,
And rest again—to ponder what is best.
You've loved me into being slow and strange,
And I give thanks and do not care to change.

Ten thousand years ago you gave us eyes
So we could slide about without surprise,
But slow—while other folks go rushing on:
Those racing snails! That tortoise marathon!

But I give thanks for being just a Slug
Who answers all harassments with a shrug;
A little damp, a little weed to eat,
A little ooze, and, ah! my life's complete.

All praise to God, Stillpoint outside of time,
I love the comfort of your sacred slime,
I rest serene within your placid calm,
And dedicate to you this sleepy psalm.

This Grief

Tears taste like salt,
taste like the ocean,
smell like the seashore.
Why do you give us ducts for tears, Creator of All,
and salty oceans covering most of the earth?

MINDFULNESS

Grief like a heavy weight, like a stone,
like a concrete block, weighs on my shoulders,
bends me over, wears me out.

CENTERING

What is lost will never be recovered.
It once was, now it is not.
I am happy that it once was.
I weep that it is no longer.
That joy has disappeared from the earth.
The world no longer contains it.

Like a stone that sad knowledge weighs me down.
I cannot stand tall. I cannot run.
I just barely stay the course,
not give up and fall,
crushed under the weight of this grief.
You walk with me, my God, bearing the same weight,
caring as much as I do.

But is your world changed as mine is?
No, not in the same way.
You have perspective.
Give me perspective today, companioning God,
though it be painful.
It sounds like good medicine
to quell
this grief.

WORDS
OF JESUS Do not fear those who kill the body
but cannot kill the soul;
rather fear those who can
destroy both soul and body.
—*Matthew 10:28*

FROM
ANOTHER
FAITH O God,
You are mother and father,
You are friend and teacher,
You are wisdom and riches—
You are everything to me, O God above all gods.
—*Ramanuja, Fourteenth Century*

MEDITATION The best name for God, according to Aquinas, was supposedly *he who is*. That may even sound comforting and welcome to our ears. It is, however, a male-centered expression, obviously. But it does express the belief that males are made in the image of God. To express the belief that women, too, are made in the image of God, do we not need the expression, at least occasionally, *she who is*?

According to theologian and author Elizabeth Johnson, we do, and she has named her recent ground-breaking and brilliant book by that title: *She Who Is*. And just as male-referent names for God reenforce male-defined values in society, the name *she who is* has wide reenforcing effects on values prized particularly by women, and with them as symbols, by the poor, the marginalized, the meek of the earth, all who suffer oppression and disempowerment.

By saying "*she who is* cares infinitely about us all," a new tone of hope for the hopeless is sounded. God is instantly seen as someone on the side of the abused and the weak ones of this world. There has never in history been an injustice as widespread and as devastating to life and community as the devaluation of women—along with all the witch-burnings, the genital mutilation, the wife-killing, the child-murdering that marks the history of women.

She who is reigns on high, visits every rape scene, hears the cries of all the poor: something will be done about it all! Like the God of the burning bush who felt the oppression of the Hebrew slaves in Egypt, the God of women and children certainly plans a path and an exodus to freedom for all the poor.

My God, in you I put my trust,
I shall never be dishonored or disgraced,
My enemies shall never win out over me,
I shall never despair.

In you I put my trust,
Your ways are wise and just.

Help me always to know your ways, my God,
Teach me your paths.
Guide me along the way of truth,
And lead me not into illusion.

In you I put my trust,
Your ways are wise and just.

For you are the Shepherd of all my ways
And the hope of all my dreams.
For you I wait all the day long,
Keeping watch all my days.

In you I put my trust,
Your ways are wise and just.

Be mindful of your tenderness, God, my God,
And remember your steadfast love,
For they have been my life from of old
And my meditation day and night.

In you I put my trust,
Your ways are wise and just.

God, my mother and my father,
help me today to find a way
to be with someone in sorrow,
or someone in danger or depression.
Somehow let me visit them in their prison
or satisfy their hunger and thirst.
Let me share in your compassion this day.

In you I put my trust,
Your ways are wise and just.

THE CONFESSION OF A CAMEL

I've fooled the world! I've conned the history books!
They honor me as patient, tough, and cheerful,
But all along my heart's been melancholy,
Forlorn, discouraged, glum, depressed, and fearful.

I carry on, oasis to oasis,
One drink does wonders when my mood is black,
I look content—so they load tons upon me
Till one more straw would break my aching back.

They shout: I smile, and do what they require,
I hide my sadness, down the road I plod,
Through desert heat and sandstorms wild and stinging,
Hoping all roads will lead to you, my God.

I can get by without a drink of water,
I can survive what burning heat there be,
But, O Leaping Sea of Hope For All the Hopeless,
How I do thirst for just one drink from thee.

10

O Infinite Music

Peace: come to my mind, my heart,
my body, my breath.
God of Action, of speeding light
and uncountable ages of time,
how is it possible that at this moment
you attend to me—in my serenity?
Yet how could I exist if you didn't?

MINDFULNESS

Into the full human circle call us, O Infinite Music,
to where only the unfamiliar is familiar
and we finally see how different and unique each of us is.
As long as I know only my similarity to the other dancers,
I remain blinded by illusion
and deaf to the harmonies only *difference* can provide.
When each "otherness" astonishes me,
I am beginning to see and hear.

CENTERING

Still, as different as we all are, we all move alike,
together Children of the Wind,
and even I can dance along.
I was made to dance,

in fact, I *am* a dance,
more a creature made of energy and motion
than of matter.
I can hear the rhythm!
I move easily—for music was my design
and harmony is my center
and rhythm runs my heart, my stomach,
my day, my year,
and my whole life's rise and fall.

Into a full human circle call me, O Great Holiness,
call us all, all the myriad beings
that compose this throbbing, dancing earth.
The music seems infinite.
Gather us in.

WORDS OF JESUS When you refuse to see things as they are,
to what should I compare you?
You are like children sitting in a circle
and calling to one another:
"I played the pipes for you, but you would not dance."
—*Luke 7:31–32*

FROM ANOTHER FAITH Quiet are the trees;
Quiet the noisy children of the night.
At the sky's restful crest burns the noonday sun.
In my heart's temple all is silent,
worshiping You, Silent Majesty,
reviving the tranquil heart.
O Eternal, Absolute, Quiet One,
in secret stillness
fill me with silence and with soundless song.
—*Prayer of India*

MEDITATION Einstein is said to have answered the inquiry: What is the ultimate unifying explanation of the world around us? by saying he could not explain it in words but could play it on his violin. I suppose that was because any explanation of our colossal interlinked reality would have to begin from elements common to us all (the way sound is common to all music), suggest a virtually limitless scope of possibilities (like the range, rhythm, dynamics, and quality of sound), and call for an expression of awe at the achievement which our reality is (like expression in music).

Surely Einstein smiled as he spoke. Only a smile would express the immense inadequacy and incongruity of any attempt at an "explanation of the world." Yet, at moments of insight music might well come to mind. Music might even bring it to mind. There is need for something beyond mathematics, beyond science, beyond words, and music can be that utterance.

Inasmuch as each of us is a unified living animal, we could be said to be "music": we are multiple rhythms and billions of miniscule motions acting as one, that is, in harmony. We are song, we are symphony. The trick is to so live as to bring our personal music into harmony with our earthen Mother's song and the whole throbbing cosmos. For that demanding task, not just any tune will do.

Finding our own tune: that's the trick. So we listen—to ourselves—for a change.

Sing to God a new song,
Sing to God, all the earth,
Sing to God, bless God's name,
Tell of God's rescue from day to day.

The earth is in song,
Let me sing along.

Declare God's glory among the nations,
God's marvelous works among all the peoples,
For great is God, and greatly to be praised,
Greatly to be honored above all gods.

The earth is in song,
Let me sing along.

Let the sky be glad, and the earth rejoice,
Let the sea roar, and all that fills it,
Let the fields exult with everything that grows.
Then all the trees of the forest shall sing for joy.

The earth is in song,
Let me sing along.

For God is coming, coming to judge the earth.

God will judge this world with justice
And the nations of the earth with wisdom
While the faithful of the earth rejoice.

The earth is in song,
Let me sing along.

PRACTICE
FOR
TODAY

Give me renewed patience today in listening for the music in others, patient Mystery. You have shown such endless, caring patience with me; let me show the same to others.

MANTRA

The earth is in song,
Let me sing along.

PLAINCHANT OF BROTHER CICADA

I hope, dear God, my monkish tone
   gives pleasure to your ear,
I sing it for your joy alone
   though sisters sometimes hear!
At times they turn in love to me
   though I'd hoped *you'd* come near
And smile to hear my psalmody,
   so celibate and sincere.

I try to lose myself in song
   and hide my private sound,
Tucked perfectly within the long
   close phrases of a round,
Forget all care for a private voice
   in mystic joy profound,
Sing beautifully but be content,
   to be the song's background.

Our plainchant fills the echoing halls
   between the rows of trees,
Cathedraled in dark oaken stalls
   and leafy canopies,
And if our psalms bring lovers near
   and fervent devotees,
We'll leave, alas, our church careers,
   for richer harmonies.

11

Your Actions Speak

Divine, quiet Love,
excuse me for not listening enough.
In silence I start to hear:
My heart beats, my breath moves,
my eyes blink, then close.
Then I watch the flow of my thoughts.
Alert I rest.

MINDFULNESS

In the things you do, Holy God,
I read your answers to my prayers,
your response to my attempts to communicate with you.
Let me put before us today your actions
for they are the only answers to my prayers
I ever expect to receive,
and I should not be surprised
that you do not answer in words or miracles
for all your actions are miracles enough.

CENTERING

Yes, here is what your voice says in answer to my prayers:
    Have air to breathe, you say,
    have eyes to see with,

have ears and words and friends with utterance and song,
have music in the air,
have children and their friends,
have feet for dancing,
have a devoted friend—or two,
have food and drink,
have the pleasure of eating,
have all the multiplex parts of human life,
have pain with healing,
have sorrow and mystery,
have death—with hope,
have prophets with vision,
have a spinning round earth home,
    with all its countless waves of energy,
    over eons, in awesome variety,
have its playgrounds and astonishing wonders,
have uncountable animal and insect companions,
    like yourself, metaphors of the Holy Mysterious,
have glowing skies, dawns, and sunsets, gleaming stars,
have emerald green, sapphire blue,
    ruby red, pearl, silver,
have taste: grape, apple, coffee, lemon,
have all lovely human linking,
have feelings of affection—with forgiveness
    and encouragement,
have love that co-creates children,
have heartbreak and anguish,
have strengthening companions,
have disappointment and error,
have myth and metaphor, analogy and paradigm,
have endless illusion,
have prophetesses and leaders,
have history and wisdom,
have books and talk,
have your life, your pain, your triumphs,
have promises.
I hear you, Mystery Beyond the Mysterious,
I give thanks.

WORDS OF JESUS   A good measure, pressed down, shaken together,
running over, will be put into your lap;

for the measure you give
will be the measure you get back.
                    —*Luke 6:38*

O God, I love the scent of the air today,
straight from your mysterious inner courts,
the scent of new perfumed garments on the garden
healing us all.
I join the trees in their worship,
the birds in their praise,
the new blue violets in their yielding.
                    —*Rumi of Persia*

Should we thank God for the good things that happen to us? Most would say yes. We give thanks that we live in a world where there is so much good luck for so many, and where some of the luck comes our way. God enters that joy with us, and enjoys whatever we enjoy, and is pleased when we realize that mystery, when we acknowledge our divine companion and creator.

Should we grimace at God when bad things happen to us? Does our bad luck mean God is punishing or abandoning us? Hardly. God also suffers with us—in some way—the bad luck, the accident, the gratuitous violence. And we can assume that God wants us to know that we are not alone.

But why the randomness, why the good and bad luck in this world, why the role of chance and of coincidence? Here we put our hand over our mouth, and like Job, surrender, yield. It's beyond us. When Job wanted an answer to Why? God said to Job: "Where were you when I laid the foundations of the earth? Who pent up the sea behind closed doors...when all the stars of the morning sang for joy? Can you unfasten the harness of the Pleiades?"

That was enough answer for Job. He said, "I put my hand over my mouth... ."

So we cannot question God about luck. It's an inexplicable phenomenon. It can't mean what it seems at first to mean: God's favor or disfavor. It is a mystery we are asked to live with—for the time being.

Stand by me, Faithful Spirit,
For I have walked in faithfulness,
Stand by me, God of my heart,
I have trusted you without wavering.

God north, God south, God east and west,
Beyond, within: your way is best.

Test me, Holy One, and try me,
Test my heart and test my mind,
For your steadfast love is before my eyes
And I walk in faithfulness.

God north, God south, God east and west,
Beyond, within: your way is best.

**PRACTICE
FOR
TODAY**

Today, Holy God, help me to be more decisive in not judging others, and more compassionate with offenders. Open my mind and heart to understand that though evil abounds, grace and graciousness do more abound.

MANTRA

God north, God south, God east and west,
Beyond, within: your way is best.

TO LIGHTEN YOUR HEART

THE CREDO OF A COCKROACH

All glory, praise and gratitude, creator of bugs supreme,
For giving me a cockroach self, with admirable self esteem.

My flattened back, my leathery shine, my tough and slippery breast,
My bristling legs all grace and speed—Oh, how I'm truly blest!

Give me due pride in who I am, my longevity and might,
If some dislike or envy me: they've got a problem, right?

Just to exist is beautiful, without added need to please.
Should I go wrong, I'll try again, then cease my apologies.

For my part I rejoice in life, modeled, Great God, on thee,
Living my low but glorious role, with joyous fertility.

What Shall
I Call You?

Do I know myself?
Beneath the names people give me,
beneath the memories
of how I've been treated, graded, and cared for,
do I know who I am, know my true name?
What is your name for me?
What should be my name for you?

MINDFULNESS

My God, are you "the Lord?"
No. You are not the Lord—
not the Lord Yahweh,
not the Lord Buddha,
not the Lord Vishnu,
not the Lord Yeshua.

CENTERING

My God, holy Creating God of all time and space,
and heaven and earth,
Vital Force behind everything
that is and moves and grows,
there was a place and a time
when "Lord" was a good-enough name for you,

to express your primacy
above the multiple gods of other nations,
to state your primacy above the forces of evil.

If at one time and in some places
we humans called you the comforting name "Lord"
(for it suggests a protecting presence
if also a demanding one),
I rejoice to realize now
that that name is no longer appropriate
for it implies "masculine" and "dominance,"
and we know you are not masculine
(nor anything partial)
and you do not so much dominate
as inhabit earthly things,
empowering each to be and to "go,"
and to be itself.
You wonderfully contain everything
like a maternal womb.

You are not my "Lord"
—you would be my companion instead.
Let me name you then by what you do:
Companion-to-us-all.

WORDS
OF JESUS

Why do you call me "Lord, Lord"
and yet not do what I tell you?
—*Luke 6:46*

FROM
ANOTHER
FAITH

Why this restless rush, this heavy sense of duty?
Your purposes stand firm.
I have one missing virtue, trust:
trust that You will meet my need.
I will rest my heavy load on You
and I, your child,
will rest serene in your sight.
This is key: You are, You are Love, You bear my cares.
—*Tukaram, Seventeenth-Century Indian Mystic*

MEDITATION

Here I am, the person you are thoroughly familiar with
as myself, another beating heart, a distractible mind, a set
of talents and limitations, a name, someone who means a

lot to you. When you hear my cry, you are here, welcome, Companioning God.

We have often erred in welcoming you: we have burned sacrifices on an altar, we have diminished ourselves, we have trembled and cowered, we have flattered and cajoled you. But none of these—except their good intentions—interested you, though you may have sometimes wept at our pathetic and pathological mistakes.

To harmonize with you, Sacred Music, to rhyme with you, Holy Word, to dance beside You, Rhythm Within Reality: this is your desire for us, for me.

Welcome, Unbelievable Partner God. With You I will walk, dance, sing, speak, today. You are acquainted with all my sorrows. You know well my limitations, my scars, and my wounds; but you know also my transcendent call, my yearning for connection with others, my precious and interdependent selfhood, my true name. Speak to me, sing to me. Here I am!

I have waited for God with patient heart
And God bent down and heard my cry,
And sent a song into my mouth,
A joyous song of thanks and praise.

You're in my blood and bones, my heart and mind,
And I'm in you, Creator, wise and kind.

You did never desire burnt sacrifice,
But you gave me instead a listening heart,
Oblations and gifts you never asked.
Then I uttered the words: Behold I come!

You're in my blood and bones, my heart and mind,
And I'm in you, Creator, wise and kind.

In the front of the book they wrote of me:
To do your will, it is my joy!
And all you ask, my living God,
Shall be a law within my heart.

You're in my blood and bones, my heart and mind,
And I'm in you, Creator, wise and kind.

I have told the Glad News here before all,

And never will I doubt your healing love,
You healed my heart, my inmost heart,
Then I uttered the word: Behold I come.

You're in my blood and bones, my heart and mind,
And I'm in you, Creator, wise and kind.

PRACTICE
FOR
TODAY Companion-To-Us-All-God, let me rely on you today to take the absurdity out of the many bewildering occurrences I will face. You will be with me through them all. Help me to remember this, and fill my heart with thanks for your unspeakable goodness.

MANTRA You're in my blood and bones, my heart and mind,
And I'm in you, Creator, wise, and kind.

TO LIGHTEN YOUR HEART

THE PRAYERFUL QUERY OF A TALL BUG

Should people call me "Daddy?" and "Longlegs?" Is it right?
Creator Wisdom, people call me that!
But "Abba"—which means "daddy"—was Jesus' name for you!
Aren't you inclined to take offense thereat?

Perhaps it shows affection when nicknames come your way,
And "Daddy Longlegs" fits the legs I've got:
The "Daddy" means I'm harmless, my legs *are* extra long,
And there are eight of them, that's quite a lot.

But you, Supreme Creator: is it appropriate
To nickname you as Jesus dared to do?
Are you a harmless Abba? A caring Oma too?
Or ought we fear the very thought of you?

You see me here before you, forgive me if today
My prayer is just this philosophic song:
With you I'll feel contented and more than pleased to be
Not feared—though we're both great, with legs quite long.

Anxiety Surrounds Me

Submersed in air and breathing it,
unconscious of the many mini-electrical events
successfully happening in my body-self
unbeknownst to me,
but not without careful shepherding,
I, one of the earth's billions of animals,
turn Godward.

MINDFULNESS

Divine Dynamic Friend Unseen,
Mystery Everywhere,
who made a world
where you yourself could hide almost perfectly,
anxiety surrounds me with its cloud,
worry grips me in her thin arms,
the brown infection of disquiet invades my bones.

CENTERING

Come, break through the darkness of my anxieties
like a bright probe of life-giving sunshine,
a surprise touch of warmth on my back,
like the promise on the face
of a mischievous bright child,
or the symphony of color
in a rising sun.

Though I belong to this threatened nation,
the human race,
and in my backpack are mandatory dread,
depression, and restlessness,
along the lonely road of inevitable pain
and stalking failure,
still I choose to hold my head high, to look to you:
ahead, above, and standing under all that will be.
That will be enough, I'm sure of it,
to hold me over till this cloud is gone.
Your compassionate presence feels all I feel
along with me, and in our sadness
we say Yes to life, such as it is.

WORDS OF JESUS

Which of you, by being anxious, can add
one single hour to your span of life?
If you can't do that, why would you
worry about anything else?

—Luke 12:25

FROM ANOTHER FAITH

O Holy Sun,
birds spring from their nests
and lift their wings in your praise.
All animals leap to their feet,
all winged things fly, then land—
all things come to life with your rising.
As your rays reach into the emerald water,
fish leap up in the river before your face.
You who create the semen in man,
it is you who guide the seed into woman.
It is you who give breath to all your creation.

—Pharoah Akhenaten, Third Century BCE

MEDITATION

The recipes from which this world has been made are amazingly improbable. The cook that created this cosmic stew: Should she be complimented or criticized?

Take marriage. Whereas we would think that "handsome man + pretty woman" is the cultural core menu for a good marriage, it doesn't work out that way very often. "Scarred man + wounded woman" is in fact the way it usually starts. If the lovers are willing to accept all the woundedness, especially their own, something wonderful can be cooked up.

Or take religion. Whereas we would think that the formula "God makes rules + humans obey" is the one that works, something quite different and unexpected is the truth: "God hides + humans search" is what we find when religion works—and add "while humans search and find themselves and each other."

Finally, take moods and feelings: elation and depression. Whereas one would think "success + good feelings" would be the normal pattern, instead we find extraordinary luck and success can lead us to moods of depression and guilt, while hard, physical work is good therapy for depression. What's going on in the kitchen?

I raise up my eyes to the hills.
From whence does my help come?
My help comes from the God of my life
Who made the heavens and earth.

You've cared for me, dear God, since life began,
I trust you help me every way you can.

God will not let my footing be lost,
The Compassionate One will not slumber.
Behold, the God who protects the oppressed
Will neither lie down nor sleep.

You've cared for me, dear God, since life began,
I trust you help me every way you can.

God is my help, my hope against hope,
A protection on my right hand.
The sun shall not strike me down by day,
Nor the moon do me harm by night.

You've cared for me, dear God, since life began,
I trust you help me every way you can.

The God of life will keep me from harm
And will rescue my soul from destruction.
God's arm will protect my comings and goings
From this time forth and forever.

You've cared for me, dear God, since life began,
I trust you help me every way you can.

PRACTICE
FOR
TODAY In pain, Divine Friend Unseen, knowing that I am made for joy and not distress, I will believe this day that peace of soul and body is on its way, and I will look to you to share all my anxieties.

MANTRA You've cared for me, dear God, since life began, I trust you help me every way you can.

THE ANGST OF A WATERBUG

Great God, have mercy on this waterbug,
And take away my soul's complete despair.
You give me luscious lilies for a home
But I must walk on water to get there!

Like Peter, I'm a soul of little faith,
I'm terrified to step where I may sink,
Yet living on the water is my life,
And risk and danger are my food and drink.

I'm cursed with existential dread and fear,
My days are spent uneasy and harassed,
I tremble overburdened with the thought
That every step I take may be my last.

I'd love to live as carefree as the lark
And dance lightheartedly along the shore
If faith to walk on water you but grant,
I promise I won't bug you anymore.

14

My Scars

With all my saints around me,
all of them made of the same clay as myself—
and all my loved ones close to my heart,
and all my enemies blessed,
I am before you, Amazing God,
Compassonate All-Wise Healer.

MINDFULNESS

O Holiness who knows me as I am,
a battered veteran of many uphill struggles,
trying to get up there where I can see,
up where I can breathe, up where I can rest:
Scarred from fighting losing battles
with sexism, racism, capitalism,
(or that ritualization of capitalism called competitiveness),
I readily come clean before you: I am scarred.
You see the scars.
The marks these evils have made on me are permanent:
Like all North American men,
these "isms" are in my bones,
in my flesh, in my blood.
Though in my head I know better,

CENTERING

my gut tells me a man is superior to a woman,
a white is superior to a person of color,
an owner is better than any employee,
an American lives more humanely than anyone else.
It follows, of course, Creating God,
that you are best analogized
as male, as white, as an owner and a lord,
and maybe even a little prejudiced in favor of Americans
("the most religious people on earth").

My scars: they are not pretty.
They look disfiguring—to those with eyes to see,
sometimes even I catch a glimpse of them
as they are—and I cringe.
So stupid I can be, so shortsighted, so prejudiced,
so self-limiting, so ignorant, doltish,
dangerous, crude, vicious;
and actions built on my scarred attitudes
are so often rude, hurtful, clumsy, and violent.
Beneath these scars is the immune-system defect
called shaming:
that makes the whole of life one vast contest,
drives its victims to think they are nothing
until they do something great,
get some high score from an educational system,
measure up to the winners or the canonized saints.

Let your grace, Never-Fathomed Mystery,
mend my defects and heal me.

WORDS
OF JESUS

Am I not allowed to do what I choose with what belongs to me? Or are you envious because I am generous?
The last will be first, and the first last.

—*Matthew 20:15–16*

FROM
ANOTHER
FAITH

As a fish dragged from the water gasps,
so my soul gasps for you.
As one who buried a treasure
and now cannot find the place,
so my soul is distraught.
As a child that has lost its mother,
so am I troubled, my heart burning with anguish....

O merciful God, you know my need.
Come, rescue me, if you can.
Show me your power and your love.
—*Tukaram, Seventeenth-Century Indian Mystic*

Because we are created for love, we are all vulnerable to shaming, to the withholding of love and respect.

When love is withheld, our human nature gets desperate, blushes, can't think, can't stand it. This is especially true of the young. We will do almost anything to restore the love. We cannot survive without it. It is a matter of life and death. And we yield to our culture which allures us, offers us artificial love, and promises false cures for our scars.

But it is only God, who is Mystery beyond what we can fathom, who cures us and heals us.

God can mend the defects in our guts and in our bones, the false images in our eyes, the twists in our pre-conditioned shamed reactions. We have to re-teach ourselves all over each day: males, whites, owners, Christians, Americans are not superior people, but are usually weak-eyed, illusion-prone, wounded, and needy.

God help us as we struggle to learn these things.

O God, I have no prayers today,
My eyes are not raised high,
I do not expect to unravel mysteries
Too great and too perplexing for me.

My heartbeat is my prayer.
My answer: You are there.

Instead I have calmed and quieted my inmost self
Like an infant quiet at its mother's breast.
Like a child in the comfort of its father's arms,
I am at peace.

My heartbeat is my prayer.
My answer: You are there.

O Holiness who knows me as I am,
show me this day how to hate wrongdoing
but still care for the culprit, even if it be me myself.

MANTRA

My heartbeat is my prayer.
My answer: You are there.

A WASP'S DISCRETE CONTRITION

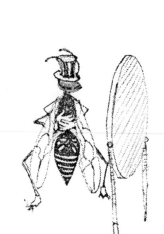

Forgive my snobbery, Great God of All,
My stinging, brusque, unmitigated gall,
My bouts of arrogance and condescension,
And frequent sins of pride too great to mention.

I'm named a "Wasp"—of that I should protest,
Mnemomic for Wee Agile Stinging Pest.
Still I give thanks I'm not like other bugs,
A cut above the rest, for all their snubs.

My special world of privilege and blood
Expects I'll build God's kingdom out of mud,
So this I do, as one of the elite,
Rich, pious, noble, proud, and most discreet.

You do forgive "pride justified," now don't you?
You'll make us sheep at your Last Judgment, won't you?
We feed the hungry—when it's in our power,
We serve the thirsting drinks at any hour,
If any Wasps are snobbish, we disown them.
If there are flaws among us, we bemoan them.

One prayer we call ahead to your Great Phone Room:
Might we reserve front pews in Heaven's Throne Room?

15

I Turn To You

Where am I?
I'll never know. Well, maybe eventually.
Am I alone? Probably not. Certainly not.

MINDFULNESS

I turn to you, Loving Mystery, Center of Creation,
and away from what is not loving
and what is not mysterious:
the evil, the twisted, and the heartless,
the cold touch of limitation, of pain,
of scientific numbers.
You will take me today, if I will go,
into love and into mystery
where I know people care for me,
and where there are no answers
to the apparent randomness of evil.

CENTERING

Take me there, dear God, it is the "real."
I have had enough of the unreal,
the unfeeling, the shell of life.
Give me connection to everyone around me,
reaching out to feel their hands,

to touch their hearts as they touch mine,
to know in their touch
that I am valuable, lovable, precious,
and to let my heart go out to them,
to where their beauty shines.

Give me rootedness in my own memories, too,
to the child I was
and still am somewhere at my core,
to the vulnerable and wide-eyed youngster,
laughing, hiding tears, learning.
Give me rootedness in Mother Earth
who has surrounded me from the very beginning
with nurturing winds of air,
with moistening clouds, wonderful to see,
white, gray, blue, promising the rain we all drink.
You surround my feet with an earth
full of its own vitality,
and hold me to it with mysterious forces,
while Earth spins through space,
a satellite circling the sun,
in a galaxy of other suns,
all of us plummeting through the cosmos,
part of a Mother Galaxy we call the Milky Way,
and part of a yet more gigantic school of galaxies.
I turn to you,
Creator of everything vast or minuscule,
and rest in your Mystery.

WORDS OF JESUS

Who are my mother and my brothers?
Whoever does the will of God
is my brother, and sister, and mother.
—Mark 3:33, 35

FROM ANOTHER FAITH

Mother Earth, Father Sky,
We are your children.
From our labor we bring you gifts that you love.
In return we pray you weave us a bright garment:
the warp, the white light of morning,
the weft, the red light of evening,
the fringes, falling rain,

the borders, the gallant rainbow.
May we walk fittingly
where grass is truly green,
Mother Earth, Father Sky.

—*Tewa Pueblo Prayer (adapted)*

MEDITATION

Something wonderful happens when we meet someone like ourselves, whatever that likeness may be: a common family tree, a passion for reading we share, a religious heritage. The quickest links come when it is a shared plight, a comparable woundedness, or a common enemy. In the circle of pain, hoops of steel are quickly forged and are tough ties to break, strong bonds we can depend on. Why is that?

Every single human person is, in important ways, "wretched, pitiably poor, blind and naked" (Revelation 3:17), and that is one commonality we can reach to whenever we encounter strangers. Then, once a bond of pain is forged, we can explore the lightsome side: common enthusiasms, common convictions, common appreciations. Differences will stick out, of course, when strangers meet, but, given deeper commonalities, differences only add color and intrigue to life. Anchored in a yearning for solidarity, if we are willing to take the risks involved, brotherly, sisterly, almost familial bonds can be forged with others.

PRAYING WITH PSALM 148

Bless God from the heavens,
Bless God in the heights.
Bless God, all angels,
Bless God, living spirits.
Bless God, sun and moon,
Bless God, shining stars.
Bless God, highest heavens,
And you waters above the heavens.

Creating God who makes us ever new,
Like embryos, we have our life in you.

Bless God from the earth, you kings and all peoples,
Princes and all rulers of the earth,

Young men and maidens together,
Old men and children.
Let all bless the name of God,
For God's name alone is exalted
With glory above earth and heaven.

Creating God who makes us ever new,
Like embryos, we have our life in you.

PRACTICE FOR TODAY Today, dear God, give me connection to everyone around me. Let me reach out to feel their hands, to touch their hearts as they touch mine. In so doing, let me rest in your Mystery this day.

MANTRA Creating God who makes us ever new,
Like embryos, we have our life in you.

TO LIGHTEN YOUR HEART

THE SPIDER'S SURRENDER

Behold, we spin our webs at your command
And frighten humans who don't understand
We are but "catching dinner," to be blunt.
They do the same—at every restaurant.

Those humans frighten us too—by their size,
Their hair, their fingered hands, their ears, their eyes,
The way they run, then peer from side to side,
Intent on unrelenting spidercide.

Oh, teach us not to dread the otherness
You've built into your world, Great Creatress,
For instance, for us eight legs are a must,
Yet some have two, or twelve! One must adjust.

We'll love them: woman, man, or octopus,
However dreadful they may seem to us.

God of Death

God of all tears,
we reach out for meaning as naturally as we breathe.
Holy Spirit, Fresh Air,
Bracing Wind from who knows where,
support us through sorrow unto joy again.

MINDFULNESS

God of Mystery and Death,
presiding every instant
over the mystery of the ending of human life,
able to see each dying one's life as a whole:
the infant in its mother's arms,
the fledgling in its father's eyes,
the days that went by one by one,
each day twenty-four hours long,
each hour containing sixty long minutes of life,
ended now, brought to an end:
No more days of life.
We've had our roughly 30,000 if we are lucky.

CENTERING

God of each death, of each whole life,
we are silent in your presence
and we look squarely at your mystery: death.

How foolish our illusion that we are immortal.
How important the dark revelation that death brings:
Life is temporary, life is often short,
almost always seems short—but life is rich.

So there is a measure of gratitude
in our hearts at death for all those minutes
when a beloved one enriched our own days.
For the privilege of celebrating this finale
with the circle of believers
who believed in this life
and who believe in this death,
that it is itself temporary,
that it is safely in the hands of God
and therefore full of meaning
though we may not know that meaning.
God of Death and of Life,
we give you our trust.

WORDS OF JESUS

Unless a grain of wheat falls into the earth and dies,
it remains alone; but if it dies, it bears much fruit.

—*John 12:24*

FROM ANOTHER FAITH

All-knowing, guiding ancestors,
O dear innocent departed ones, hear our voices,
you are not blind nor deaf to this life we live,
you shared it yourselves.
Be a good help to us now,
for we do not forget you.

—*West African Prayer*

MEDITATION

One way to see Jesus' death as messianic and salvific is to conjure up some kind of theological need for death. Is that not what St. Paul did? Paul, for all his ecstatic wisdom on other topics, seemed to assume—with his contemporaries—that God wanted a colossal human sacrifice to placate the divine justice for the sins of the world. This was a mentality familiar in the ancient world: God is fearsome and unpredictable. What can "he" want? What will make him happy? Well, how about the sacrifice of our most precious possessions, even of precious humans, our children? In St. Paul's theology, only the murder and sacrifice of a divine being would appease God: the perfect sacrifice. And that's how, according to Paul, Jesus saved us: We were all sinners and Jesus satisfied "all justice" in his willing death. He died for us.

But this doesn't ring true. Many theologians and philosophers alike reject it. Doesn't it make more sense to assume that the death of Jesus was like the death of any human: a necessary part of any earthly life, something as natural as the rest of life, like birth both mysterious and painful, a mystery we have to live with to the end?

Jesus, of course, did more. He took risks in confronting his times with a public criticism of the political/religious system in which he lived, and he was hunted down and executed by those whose privileges he threatened. And so he did die for others (and even for us all): in the sense that he took the risks for others.

Even if we ourselves are not called by history to take mortal risks, facing an ordinary death requires heroism. We must each die our death, and nobody can die for us. In the end our common hope is that we will feel God at our side through it all: and Jesus models that, too. He handed over his short vigorous life saying to God, "Into your hands I commend my spirit." A model death, a model for us.

M y God, in you I will put my trust,
I shall never be dishonored or disgraced,
My enemies shall never win out over me,
I shall never despair.

You who life eternal give,
If you call me, I can live.

Help me always to know your ways, my God,
Teach me your paths.
Lead me along the way of truth,
And lead me not into illusion.

You who life eternal give,
If you call me, I can live.

Be mindful of your tenderness, God, my God,

And remember your steadfast love,
For they have been my life from of old
And my meditation day and night.

You who life eternal give,
If you call me, I can live.

PRACTICE
FOR
TODAY

God of my life and of every life, may I be blessed
enough today to know how lucky I am to be alive—
and may I share this blessing with all I meet.

MANTRA

You who life eternal give
If you call me, I can live.

THE MAYFLY'S LAMENTATION

I live to die—a poor mayfly.
Why link sweet May with someone so banal?
I'll say the word! I am absurd!
I don't make sense! I have no rationale!

So difficult to grow adult,
Then, never eating, life lasts but one day,
But one short stint to shine and glint,
Then I become some trout or salmon's prey.

One shining hour within my bower
To mate, be fruitful! Ah, there's wit for gleaning!
Perhaps I'm part of larger art!
In that case even mayflies would have meaning!

Yes, I can cope, and I can hope
As long as I am linked with something greater,
Great kings must die and so must I:
The reason why, I'll leave to my creator.

Looking Back

Your vision of me:
Does it not contain all that I am and have been?
I am alive, I feel alive:
and you create all my aliveness.
I have a past also: and you remember every detail,
God of History.

MINDFULNESS

Looking back in time
and remembering the past,
we bless and praise you, dear Unimaginable God,
for you not only remember,
but also contain the past.
For one thing,
it was to you that we delivered
all our deceased loved ones.
They are now in you somehow
and your nearness makes them near as well.
We bless and give you thanks for this.

CENTERING

But, more, you also contain
all that was significant in the past,

in you is all that beauty,
all that heroism, all that ecstasy,
everything that mattered in the long run
is contained in you.
How wonderful is your presence, Endless Mystery,
containing all the past.

Looking back in time we remember
some threads of our own history,
but you remember—and contain—
the whole awesome web of it.
In you our loved ones live still,
in you they still have their being
and all the meaning of their lives endure—in you.
You contain it all.

Once I think this thought,
that nothing good in the past is lost,
then I know anew that my appetite for being is limitless,
and that I cannot live without a future.

Be close to our thoughts, Holy Creating Spirit-God,
in you is all that exists
and all that is significant of the past.
To be close to you is awesome for you contain,
like an inexpressibly wonderful cosmic womb,
all that has been, is, and will be.

WORDS OF JESUS

Abide in me as I abide in you.
Just as the branch cannot bear fruit by itself
unless it abides in the vine, neither can you unless you
abide in me. I am the vine, you are the branches.
—*John 15:4*

FROM ANOTHER FAITH

Listen, my soul,
love God as the lotus loves the water.
Buffeted by the waves, its affection does not waver.
As creatures that have their being in water,
if taken out of water, die—
so would I be apart from you.
So I would love you, God, as the lotus loves the water.

Listen, my soul,

Love God as the fish loves water.
The more the water, the greater its joy,
the greater the tranquility of its mind and body.
Out of water, only God knows the anguish of its heart.
As without water it cannot live one watch of the day—
so I would love you, God, as the fish loves the water.
—*Sikh Prayer*

Let your breath be slow and deep. Imagine that you are MEDITATION a great tree with roots extending deep into the center of Earth. Let your breath move down into your roots and, at the same time, out through your highest branches. Breathe deeply into your root. Let the energy from Earth travel through your roots and up through your highest branches, out into the sky above you. Breathe deeply. Let the light of the sun touch your branches, travel down through your trunk, deep into your roots, and flow out into Earth.

When you feel fully grounded, in touch with both Earth and the sky, become aware that in your heart/mind there exists a garden. Its fruits spring from the energy of your thoughts. As your breath sinks deep within your body, let your mind travel deep within until you find yourself in the garden of the heart. Now is the time to weed the garden, to uproot from the garden any thoughts that are limiting, any emotional patterns that are negative, any actions that are incomplete. See yourself pulling up, weeding out, those thoughts of fear, separation, scarcity, and pain. As you carefully weed the garden, take time to bring to mind the ways in which these thoughts were strangling the beautiful plants in the garden. Weed the garden, aware that these weeds, these limiting thoughts, are no longer necessary. Throw the weeds onto the compost pile so that they can be used as fertilizer to help the new seeds to grow.

When you have uprooted all the weeds, imagine yourself spreading the compost over the garden. When the soil is ready, begin to plant new seed-thoughts, affirmations of courage, abundance, and joy. Plant new seed-thoughts of well-being for yourself and for all of Earth. As each new thought is planted, let its energy resonate like a mantra through your entire being.

Safe in the garden of the mind, let the new seeds take root. Affirm that they will feed all of life. Safe in the garden of your mind, allow the seeds to take root that they may be harvested for the good of all life.

—from *The Hope for Wholeness* by Katherine Zappone

PRAYING WITH PSALM 98

In majesty are you robed, O God,
Our God is clothed in power,
And beauty too is your royal garb,
Your raiment like the rainbow.

O Beauty ever ancient, ever new,
With all that you have made, I look to you.

This world you have made unshakable, O God,
And as your throne it has stood since the beginning,
You existed transcending all from the first day,
A God who cares for all things great and small.

O Beauty ever ancient, ever new,
With all that you have made, I look to you.

Great rivers raise their voices,
Great waters raise their thunders,
Yet greater than even the voice of the ocean,
God speaks triumphant on high.

O Beauty ever ancient, ever new,
With all that you have made, I look to you.

PRACTICE FOR TODAY

Today, be close to my thoughts,
Holy Creating Spirit-God.
Remind me often that in you is all that exists
and all that is significant of the past.
Remind me, too, that my tears can be rain
on the flowerbed of my hopes.

MANTRA

O Beauty ever ancient, ever new,
With all that you have made, I look to you. ❑

18

You Have Found Me

As I try to rest from thought,
your puzzling mystery rises in my consciousness.
Do you study me, Divine Creator?
Surely I don't puzzle you
as I puzzle myself.

Here I am, Mystery of Presence,
my God, my Meaning,
you have found me.
This is prayer.
You find me even when I do not find you,
even when I am bewildered
by an avalanche of images.
So I place myself here in peace of soul
before your eyes
in the presence of all other humans.

Like the gray mist
that had its birth in your divine imagination,
like the storm approaching,
like the humming wind and all those I love,
I am before you—

so you can find me—
finding myself in the web of life
in which you've woven my being.
The silence of this hour
vibrates with your divine music.
In the darkness I feel the clear day
of your mystery.

Your love for me is written in the wind,
in the storm, in the mist.
And I have no fear,
for nothing can separate us, Giver of Hope.
I shall never be alone or left behind
or abandoned or without a home
as long as there is you—around and within me
and before me and behind me and under me.
You have found me.
So be it.

WORDS OF JESUS Even the hairs of your head are all numbered, so don't be afraid of anything. You are of great value.

—Matthew 10:30–31

FROM ANOTHER FAITH From this moment, do with me as you will.
My mind is one with your mind. I am yours.
I turn down nothing that seems good to thee.
Send me wherever you will. Clothe me as you will.
If it is your will, I take office or live privately,
remain at home or live in exile, be poor or rich.
I will, in all of these, stand with your purpose.

—Epictetus, First Century

MEDITATION Centering, communicating with God at one's center, can be—as it is in this book—a serious conversation with the Divine Mystery; or it can be wordless: a dance, a hum, or a posture. It cannot be a trick, a feat, a privilege, or a commodity. It should never be a bore, an ordeal, an expense, or a self put-down.

Communicating with God is sometimes called prayer. But it is not so important what we call it: it's good to do. A better word for it is "centering" because God is at our center. But we don't need any particular name for it—or any words at all.

For believers, centering always involves communicating with God, and it is natural and easy and happens in a flash. To imply that communicating with God must take a good chunk of time, or requires sophisticated knowledge, or is facilitated by the services of professional holy people, or is some kind of vigorous and painful climb that can be calibrated into higher and higher styles—is very misleading.

It is especially misleading to think that any kind of prayer is "a process of interior purification leading, if we consent, to union," a definition of something called *centering prayer*. What's eccentric about that description is that it implies the tiresome illusion that we're full of something impure and in constant need of purification. And it implies that to be superior pray-ers, we need the leisure that only privileged people have. Not true.

Jesus of Nazareth's prayers can be models for us, and he is depicted as praying to God very often, both alone and with friends. He never described his solitary prayer for us, so we don't have any particular detailed way to follow. Freedom therefore is the ultimate rule for disciples of Jesus. We can follow our own instincts. God is no distance away, is easy to find. Center yourself. God will find you.

This earth is God's with all its wealth,
This world and those who dwell therein;
For God has set it on the sea,
And built it on the waters underneath the earth.

Ocean of Life, whose depths we'll never know,
All things are yours and toward you all things flow.

Who shall ascend the hill of God?
Who stand in God's most holy place?
Those with open hands, those with new hearts,
Those who love the truth and walk in honest promises.

Ocean of Life, whose depths we'll never know,
All things are yours and toward you all things flow.

They will be blest by heaven's care,
And touch the morning's innocence,
Their searching hearts will look to God
And seek the face of each elusive Mystery.

Ocean of Life, whose depths we'll never know,
All things are yours and toward you all things flow.

Mystery of Presence, my God, my Meaning, may I be so turned on by life today that I endure hardship almost without noticing it, and defer gratification as a matter of course. Help me to believe that I shall never be alone as long as there is you—around and within me.

Ocean of Life, whose depths we'll never know,
All things are yours and toward you all things flow.

THE MURMUR OF A MICROBE

Ocean of Oozing Life from whom I came,
I know your throbbing force but not your name,
I know in faith you're good and wondrous wise,
And I'm your image, though I'm small in size.
(If I ten thousand times were magnified
I'd still not be one inch from side to side.)

Microbes are small—with no need to be first,
But not without a job—(which is the worst
That little folks can suffer, I am told),
But our role's clear, our functions manifold.
At all our worldwide tasks we are the whizzes,
We're Algae, Protozoans, Virusizzes,
Mold, Germs, Bacteria—a noble clan.
We were primordial life when life began.

We're everywhere, and even live within
All living beings' veins, organs, and skin,
And when we die, we lie down without grief
And form a Dover cliff, a coral reef.
We're joyful, God, great Creatress of all,
To be significant, however small.

78

Let's Be
Born Again

Thinking of the child within me,
is there any of that child left?
What good instincts that child had!
Does not our God—dwelling outside of time—
still know that child very well?

MINDFULNESS

God of a Three-fold Overflowing Communion,
Unimaginable Mystery and Heart of Compassion,
Perfect Caring Presence and Source of all Being,
help our divided race,
which at birth you constantly create as "united"
(before "culture" begins its work of separation).
Help this divided human race
to be re-united.
Our divisions, like terrible wounds,
are so painful and so weakening and so dangerous:
separating black from white, woman from man,
child from adult, gentile from Jew,
Catholic from Protestant, rich from poor,
Hindu from Moslem, labor from capital,

CENTERING

weak from powerful,
making all the world a battleground.

Can you bring about a healing, starting with myself?

Now that we are one global village,
and no group can be left out,
no individual forgotten or lost,
now that history has made us all newsworthy,
all one human family,
can you make us somehow one "culture?"

Is there any way we all can rise above our divisions
or dig below our foundational differences,
or outflank our implacable defenses
and diverse languages
and be re-united as we all were at birth,
as you made us?
Can we all be born again—without prejudices?

WORDS OF JESUS Unless we are born anew,
we cannot enter the realm of God.
—John 3:3

FROM ANOTHER FAITH O God, let us humans stand united,
Let our speech be harmonious,
Let our minds reach out similarly.
Common be our words to you,
Common be our purpose,
Common be our decisions,
Common be our thinking.
May our feelings be alike,
May our hearts be unified,
May our desires be similar.
May our unity be perfect.
—Hindu Prayer, First Century

MEDITATION The Eucharist is so rich a ceremony, so full of meaning
and suggestion, that Christians never tire of thinking
about it, talking about it, arguing about it—and fighting
about it. How would one explain in a short space what
the Eucharist is to, say, a member of an aboriginal tribe

who might inquire about it, knowing nothing of Christianity? Here is an attempt.

The bread and wine—which we Christians put on the Communion Table—are symbolic of all the gifts we as a community want to hand over to God: our gifts for peace and peacemaking, our gifts of body and spirit, our pledges of resources and time, and above all our personal joys, sorrows, and concerns. All this we commit into God's hands with the ritual food and drink. We then pray that these gifts of ours be transformed, to become for us the work and the presence of the Messiah in the world, the continuation of the life and work, the courage and wisdom, of Jesus of Nazareth.

Next we prayerfully recount that our prophet, on the night before he was captured and executed, when he was celebrating the Jewish Passover with his friends, at one point took the bread and broke it up and gave pieces of it to his disciples to eat, saying: here, take and eat this bread, the bread of affliction which at Passover we set aside for the poor—this is my body, my self, my soul, all my resources; I want you to make it your food. Share together—and with the whole world—my gospel. The disciples then ate that bread, surely bemused, caught by the symbolism. ("Yes, he gave himself totally to us and to his times and to his nation.")

Likewise when supper was ended Christians recall how Jesus, according to the scriptures, took a cup full of wine and ritualized a covenant—the kind of blood-sealed agreement that many nations were familiar with—but a covenant between earth and heaven, between humankind and God. He said, "This wine is my blood, the blood of a new covenant with God. Take this, all of you, and drink of it"—implying that in tasting the wine they were each ratifying the new covenant.

Therefore in our bread and wine ceremony, re-enacted frequently among Christians, is the remembrance of Jesus, and the dedication to carry out what the ritual symbolizes: "Be you as generous with your life as is a loaf broken and given out, as a cup of wine poured out. May you be as committed and faithful to God in this new covenant, as were your forebears. Be this way, this generous

—in memory of me."
Would the non-Christian understand?

O God most wise and all-compassionate,
O Heart unable not to look on me,
How was I ever chosen to exist?
And given being and a destiny?

You are my God, my guide,
I sense you at my side.

I entered life in fragile innocence,
My heart was clean as any windswept peak,
My lips were cleansed with kisses from the heart,
And I was taught your holy face to seek.

You are my God, my guide,
I sense you at my side.

They told me of your presence at the start
And I will honor you until I die,
For better is one day within your tent
Than years when I'm alone and know not why.

You are my God, my guide,
I sense you at my side.

O Holy God of heaven and of earth,
With joy I know your presence at my side,
I know I shall not fail or be afraid
Or lose the way—while you shall be my guide.

You are my God, my guide,
I sense you at my side.

PRACTICE
FOR
TODAY

Teach me today, Source of All Being,
to revere diversity and to enjoy making bridges,
for then my world will be large indeed.

MANTRA

You are my God, my guide,
I sense you at my side. ❏

20

God of the Future

See me, mindful God, just me,
a living thing among living things,
a creation, alive and mindful.

MINDFULNESS

Holy God, still so unknown to me and to all our race,
God of the past, the present, and especially of the future,
I welcome the future you offer me,
my future—with all it will bring.
I open my arms to it—with all its unknowns
because I can trust you, ultimately.

CENTERING

But I cannot trust you superficially.
There is undeniably a randomness in creation,
in good things and bad,
for which you can't be blamed or credited.
What I thank you for in advance
is your presence even in the zones of chaos,
that blinding light which I face daily,
that darkness that contains you—
into which I look in vain.
Throughout my whole future you will be there,

and you bring meaning to it all,
however hazily I may see it.

So I welcome the future you will have for me.
My tomorrow comes from you,
and in it I entrust myself to you:
for richer, for poorer,
in sickness and in health,
till death do us—unite.

With faith and hope I step out
on the path you have laid before me.
I welcome the revelations, the excitement,
the awesome vistas and the mysteries,
the disappointments, even the dangers
(knowing you will be there),
full of cautious confidence and trusting dread.

WORDS OF JESUS Blest are the meek, for they shall inherit the earth.
—Matthew 5:5

FROM ANOTHER FAITH Attend to this very day: it is life,
the truest life of your life.
In its brief course lie many mysteries:
bliss is one,
the splendor of beauty is another.

Yesterday is but a dream,
tomorrow is only a vision,
but this day well spent
makes every yesterday a happy dream
and every tomorrow a hopeful vision.
Attend to this very day: it is life.
—Sanskrit Prayer

MEDITATION Nothing is so silly an aim in life as holiness—if by holiness we mean anything like "unearthly," or "a cut above," or "closer to God." That kind of holiness only thrives in a universe of competition and narcissism: a male supremicist universe.

Think about the word holy. "Holy" semantically implies "otherness." It sets us apart. But to make it our aim to be "set apart" is profoundly silly because our most humane aim is to be firmly grounded somewhere, to be connected, to feel connected, to discover our connectedness. Connectedness is of our essence.

Still from our earliest days in school we find ourselves forced into competition with others. School children are "graded," as with grades of meat: grade A, grade B, grade C. Most of us have been graded and shamed from our earliest days at home as well: Be good! Behave! Don't embarrass us! The grading system works as a control. Studies show that girl babies are picked up when they cry far more quickly than are boy babies. Why? Boys must learn to compete and be tough, and to that end we ration their connectedness, tend not to pick them up. Independence, set-apartness, not inter-dependence, is soon the most prized quality. Finally, the highest competitors aim at not just success or fulfillment or integration or wholeness—but holiness. Silly.

It is meaning I thirst for, O God, My God,
And I believe that purpose and significance
Stand under all that is and all that happens.

You are the God of sky and earth,
You are the God who gave us birth.

When shall I see the design
Beneath the reality around me?
I will choose the world that is,
Holding out for just this:
That meaning stands under all that happens,
That absurdity does not prevail ultimately.

You are the God of sky and earth,
You are the God who gave us birth.

My tears have been my food day and night,
My enemies ridicule me:
Where is that God of his, people ask.

You are the God of sky and earth,
You are the God who gave us birth.

Today, Holy God, help me to laugh at the egocentric thoughts that float to the surface of my mind. This habit of seeing myself at the world's center is a stigmatism I must learn to cope with. Teach me how.

You are the God of sky and earth,
You are the God who gave us birth.

THE ANTHEM OF THE GIRAFFE

All laud to Thee, Exalted One,
Who wondrous deeds on earth hast done,
Not least divine of which I be,
For I see far ahead, like Thee.

Like Thee, Your Highness, I am wise,
And future things are in mine eyes.
My long neck craneth high above
As I peer down with lofty Love.

When I do pray, thou art my guide,
My diction highly sanctified,
Me, Supreme Beast; Thou, Supreme Being,
We oft confer, always agreeing.

Thank God I'm not as others be,
Earthbound and gross, of low degree.
Instead I soar divinely high,
Not made for earth! Part of the Sky!

21

No Time For Anything

I will take time,
I will concentrate my thought and feeling at my center,
remaining connected there to all those I care about.

MINDFULNESS

Where did I get the idea
that there is no time for anything?
How did I get brainwashed into dreaming
that I am relentlessly chased by someone,
or chased by some machine
that shreds all I've accomplished
and shouts out tasks I must do
but will never get around to:
people who will die if I don't discover a way to feed them,
worthy agencies of compassion
teetering on the brink of failure,
depending on my continued support;
books I must begin to read today
so I can be useful, not look foolish, tomorrow;
tasks that will never get done
unless I personally do them—soon.

CENTERING

I am chased—by an importunate ego—
my soul harried in the spinning squirrel cages
that trap my imagination.
Arrogance (so much depends on me!)
terrifies me if I do not face it down—
which takes time.

So this minute I'll take time.
First let me rest awhile
in your dynamic peacefulness, Holy God.
Then I will accept what is real around me:
maybe the woods can tell me that,
maybe I'll study the lake:
how it makes music deep below
and all round its edges and over its surface,
how it sleeps.
Are there stars out there?
Yes, all night and all day.
Then with stars in my eyes
I'll take my place in the drama
but only read my own lines,
not those of other players,
not get into the act on stage
when my place is in the wings.

Next I'll be content to make the unique sounds
that I'm in the drama to make,
self-possessed—instead of driven—
collected, not scattered,
composed, not pulled apart:
my better, unhurried, real self.

WORDS OF JESUS Come to me all you who are weary
and are carrying heavy burdens, and I will give you rest.
Take my yoke upon you, and learn from me;
for I am gentle and humble in heart,
and you will find rest for your souls.

—Matthew 11:28–29

FROM ANOTHER FAITH Grant me the aptitude to be alone:
each day to be outdoors a little while alone
among the trees and grasses,

among all that grows,
and to stay there alone and enter into prayer,
to talk with the one
to whom I belong.
                    —*Rabbi Nachman of Bratzlav*

Without a God, there is never enough time, and life is MEDITATION ultimately a futile pursuit of life. Without a God, there is never enough meaning, and life is largely absurd. Without a God, there will never be enough justice, and life becomes a drama of crushing inequality.

When we decide to believe in God, we choose also to believe in justice, meaning, and value. And believing in these three is, for many, the same as believing in God.

Being with God and believing in God are not passive things. To rest in God means to reach out toward the fire which connects us to God.

Theologian Elizabeth Johnson says that "God is the fire of sheer aliveness whose act of being overflows, bringing the universe into existence and empowering it to be. This language carries the companion recognition that all things are on fire with existence by participation in God's holy being which is unquenchable."

Help us, dear God, we turn to you PRAYING WITH PSALM 12
For there are few who help,
So many friends have disappeared,
Gone from the human circle.

God of the real beyond my reach,
Your perfect peace and wisdom teach.

Protect us now, Most Holy God,
Guard us from every danger.
Help us, our Rock, our Guide, our Mountain,
For there are few who help.

God of the real beyond my reach,
Your perfect peace and wisdom teach.

Holy God, show me today how to spend some time PRACTICE FOR TODAY
outside of time, bonding with friends, nest-building,

and appreciating beauty wherever it may hide.
Grant me, too, "the aptitude to be alone."

MANTRA God of the real beyond my reach,
Your perfect peace and wisdom teach.

THE HURRIED HYMN OF A BUMBLING BEE

I can't slow down to sing a psalm
Except to hum,
I must stop in on rose, sundrop,
Geranium,
Forsythia, tulip, violet,
Chrysanthemum!

This yellow jacket that I wear,
This royal robe,
Opens the door to every flower
I care to probe,
To help make love between them live
Around the globe.

But I must hurry: tough, true love's
In short supply,
I have a million visits due
Before I die,
And many hearts to link before
I say goodbye.

Your name, pure being, sounds like mine,
Great hive of grace,
Pure beeing is all I can lay
Before your face:
Hurry! And we can make the world
A honeyed place.

22

I'll Save the World

This mind, this body, this history:
what am I here for
if not something grandiose?

MINDFULNESS

Mystery Most Loving,
Unimaginably Creative Spirit,
one thing you may find lovable in me:
(did you put it there?)
the impulse to save the world,
my ongoing illusion that every problem has a solution
and, given enough time, I can fix everything:
families in Brazil who live their whole lives
on garbage heaps,
AIDS victims marginalized like lepers,
children who, one day at school,
suddenly realize they're different from other kids:
being homeless;
battered women, exploited workers, abused elders.
I'll fix it all by convincing the sinfully rich
that they have to share with, and live with,
the human race,

CENTERING

winning over arrogant leaders
to compassion and dis-illusion,
politicians to single-eyed honesty,
health workers to unprofiteering service,
academics to concern for the larger questions,
the young to dedication,
the old to optimism.

Maybe I should rather strive
for the grace of intellectual realism,
and that illusive virtue of accepting defeat,
submitting to the cold facts I know,
hoping there are a million warm facts I do not know.
I am before you, Holy Wisdom,
wondering if there is a cure for me,
or if even you
can save the world.

WORDS
OF JESUS **W**hy do you worry so much today about tomorrow's problems? Tomorrow will have problems of its own. Sufficient for today is today's trouble.

—Matthew 6:34

FROM
ANOTHER
FAITH **M**ay all be beautiful before me,
May all be beautiful behind me,
May all be beautiful below me,
May all be beautiful above me,
May all be beautiful around me....

—Navajo Chant

MEDITATION **N**ot long ago we heard the news that White South Africans have finally voted to share political status with the people they call "Blacks" there. A New York Times editorial had the eloquence to say they did it out of "decency and realism."

A few inches away, on that same editorial page, it was mentioned that sixty individuals or families in the U.S. possess one billion dollars each—or more. Think about that: one thousand million dollars. Or more. That's undeniable financial obesity.

Should we not invite these sixty to immediately give up

at least half of what they own, perhaps appealing to "decency and realism"?

Give it up to whom? A group of foundations has formed "The Funding Exchange" for just that purpose. It's in the New York phone book. The Exchange is ready with information on the most deserving charities, just a phone call away. Think: those sixty American individuals or families with one billion or more would still have at least five hundred million each.

Then, if they had the decency and realism to give up the first half, how about next cutting their assets to a maximum of one hundred million? How much more decent—and realistic!

Why the word "decency" in the editorial? Because in South Africa it was only "decent" to open up their political parties to Blacks, to open up job opportunities, educational opportunities, religious communities, neighborhoods, to Blacks—because Blacks have great intellectual, industrial, and cultural riches to dedicate to building up that society, and they deserve to share in the country's wealth. It is "indecent" to keep them out of the civil process.

Why the word "realistic"? Because, of course, there was no longer any way to hold them back, short of a bloodbath involving both Blacks and Whites.

Will the day come in the U.S. when our sixty billionaires see that it's only "decent and realistic" to share some of what they have? Not until Americans are made aware of the indecency of our inequity in ownership, and are prepared to take the risks involved in demanding a fair share of the nation's bounty.

How does God feel about all this? Angry, of course. Or the divine equivalent of angry. Suppose a loving mother prepared enough food for all her family, then saw that some were not getting a decently fair share? It is not unrealistic to imagine anger in such a mother.

Holy Earth-Birthing and Mothering Spirit, give us hearts in harmony with your own. Give us hearts sick of the indecency of joblessness and destitution, and hands realistically ready to face the costs of building a multinational Common-Wealth in the future.

Unless God builds the house,
Those who build it work in vain.
Unless God watches over the city,
The watchman stays awake for nothing.

Dear God, call when I wake
so I rise for your sake.
Dear God, build when I build,
so your will be fulfilled.
Dear God, rest when I rest
so all my sleep be blest.

Unless God wakes within you,
For nothing you get up so early.
Unless God works when you labor
In vain you eat the bread of anxious toil
And go so late to bed.

Dear God, call when I wake
so I rise for your sake.
Dear God, build when I build,
so your will be fulfilled.
Dear God, rest when I rest
so all my sleep be blest.

PRACTICE FOR TODAY

Mystery Most Loving, beginning this day help me to persistently pursue worthy goals despite frequent, discouraging failure. Make my faith a wonder! Show me how to deal with today's problems today.

MANTRA

Dear God, build when I build,
so your will be fulfilled.
Dear God, rest when I rest
so all my sleep be blest. ❑

23

Unhappy With Myself

A valued body-self, a centered mind:
Why so depressed?
An illness of soul?

MINDFULNESS

So much of your creation, Communioning Spirit,
is splendidly whole:
How can I present myself before you without shame?
All the seven deadly sins have a foothold in my heart,
sloth, lust, covetousness, envy, anger, pride, greed;
and many dozen more: dishonesty, harsh judgment,
arrogance, cowardice, injustice, distrust, insensitivity,
selfishness, isolation, disbelief, self indulgence....

CENTERING

None of these defects exists in the animal world.
What we might call lust, anger, or sloth among animals
is only part of their nature,
while it should be part of our nature also to be whole—
but we aren't, obviously.

You see it so clearly, Most Wise Creator.
I can barely get along with those I care about most,

much less those I despise
and especially those I fear.
Grant me more light
in this dark little world I live in, Creator of Light.
A land of shadows seems small and mean.
Fountain of Wisdom, guide of us each and all,
I suspect a larger world would seem a happier one.

WORDS
OF JESUS

If you forgive others their debts,
your heavenly Father will forgive you yours.
—*Matthew 6:14*

FROM
ANOTHER
FAITH

God is the light of the heavens and the earth.
The light of God is like a niche
where a lamp burns in the night,
the lamp in a glass, and the glass a brilliant star.
The lamp fire is kindled from a holy tree, an olive,
the oil of which seems incandescent of itself
without the touch of fire.
God gives the oil, the lamp, the light,
then guides to the light the chosen ones....
—*Muslim Meditation*

MEDITATION

Many illusions cloud my vision. Don't I often think of myself as the central entity in the universe? Don't I often think of myself as morally indomitable, unthreatened by the obvious brokenness and mortality of the world around me, a brokenness I can forget about and keep separate from myself? Don't I often assume that the Divine Mystery is primarily attending to me? Don't I habitually think of God as quite comprehensible—even though far away (when the exact opposite is the case: God is very close, and incomprehensible)?

Don't I usually think that my own moral system of right and wrong is applicable to other people so that I may make a moral judgment about them? In my personal moral system, is not sin really unforgivable? Is not privilege and good luck enhancing of the self? Is not everyone, especially myself, expected to function autonomously and independent of others? On any given day am I not immortal? Can I not make it my earthly aim to reach a plateau of permanent safe and contented happiness? Is the worst that can happen to us early death, disease, and injury?

Does not the Creator expect heroism of me daily, the purest of unselfish intentions, a life of unceasing work, an undistracted awareness of God, no fears or self-interest, no ego needs or infirmities, and a prayer life that includes a constant clear concept of a lovable God and interminable expressions of gratitude? Wait! Only in darkness can such illusions thrive. Who was it said "I am the light of the world"?

If you dwell in the shelter of the Most High God
And within God's shadow abide,
You can say, "I have God for a refuge and a rock,
I can trust God will take my side."

Be with me, God, when I am in trouble.
Stay at my side when I need you there.

No evil shall defeat you, or illness hold you down,
For the angels watch your nights and days.
All the messengers of heaven will be looking after you,
For they guard you in all your ways.

Be with me, God, when I am in trouble.
Stay at my side when I need you there.

With loving hands they shall carry you along,
Lest you stumble with your burdens and fears.
You shall walk unhurt on the viper and the asp,
And be fearless of the lion and his peers.

Be with me, God, when I am in trouble.
Stay at my side when I need you there.

If you turn to me, I will save your life,
You will triumph when you call my name.
If you call to me, I will answer you,
And will bring you out of danger and shame.

Be with me, God, when I am in trouble.
Stay at my side when I need you there.

Today, Most Wise Creator,
I will try to believe in my own life,
despite any disappointment or grief.
This act of faith is an important one for me.

MANTRA

Be with me, God, when I am in trouble.
Stay at my side when I need you there.

THE DRAGONFLY'S DEPRESSION

Ancient Wisdom Ever New!
Behold your creature, feeling blue,
Depressed, disheartened, cheerless, down,
With somber eyes and joyless frown.

I'm made to fly and levitate
While in my arms I hold my mate,
She loves to soar and dive and race
For miles and miles in my embrace.

Instead, a gloom pervades my heart,
My energies refuse to start,
And why? No reason: just the weight
Of life and death and pain and fate.

Great God of life, your way is best,
I know at heart my life is blest,
So I'll endure this night of gloom
Till morning flowers start to bloom.

Meantime I'll keep faith undefiled
And hope—because I'm Wisdom's child—
For all the joy and inner glow
That flying dragons ought to know.

If I Were You

As I pull myself together,
stars burn a colossal distance above,
the iron core of the earth boils 800 miles down,
my heart beats on and on,
my body-self rests,
my eyes close to illusion,
and I awake to the real.

MINDFULNESS

If I were you, Infinitely Resourceful Creator,
the *first thing* I would do would be
to remove physical pain from the world.
What a sigh of relief we would breathe worldwide!

CENTERING

The *second thing* I would do would be to make
everyone beautiful to everyone else.
That would end hatred, and multiply love and joy.

The *third thing* I would do would be to make you
visible, audible, and undeniable,
so our race would be fundamentally reverent and thankful,
and in turn, generous with one other.
All would worship you without ceasing.

Next I would eliminate hunger and disease, and death as we know it: unpredictable, often lingering. One would die when it felt like the right moment: press a button, you're gone. Into heaven.

Then I would provide for and guarantee excellent coupling. Everyone would enjoy all that goes with a good marriage: fascinating mutuality, the joys of sexual love and intimacy, then the thrills of childbearing—and the children would all be healthy and promising. I would do these things and so much more.

God of wisdom and might,
why can't the world be this way?
I really don't understand why it can't.
Are you really unable to do these things,
or do you just choose not to?
Are we not allowed to ask you about this?
Or ...is life about something other than being happy?

WORDS OF JESUS After tasting old wine, people don't want new wine. They say: The old is good.   *—Luke 5:39*

FROM ANOTHER FAITH Let me walk in beauty,
Great Spirit who speaks in the wind,
who breathes life into all the world.
Though I am small and weak,
I need your power and wisdom.
Let me walk in beauty
and may my eyes ever feast on
the red and purple sunset.
Let my hands reverence all you have made
and my ears be quick to hear your voice.
Give me wisdom to understand
all you have taught my people,
to learn the lessons hidden in every leaf and rock....
                    —Native American Prayer

MEDITATION When times are financially tight for me, my pile-up of unanswered envelopes from needy organizations gets thicker and thicker: they all touch and move my heart strings. Half these "prayers" that come my way end up discarded, the others fatten up my agenda file, waiting. Usually I decide one day what I can afford, and send them all a small check, hoping to help them stay alive by getting a little from many. But I never feel quite right about it all.

Lately I have been wondering if God may be in the same fix, and be similarly in agony about it—because surely God understands and sympathizes with every prayer we utter. And surely that Divine Love has for us all some kind of impossible wish or other—for instance, that more prayers could be simply and specifically "answered": really heal our sorrows, really save us from pain, really guide us with unmistakable inspiration. And then God must agonize at least a little, knowing such "answers" are really not possible in the larger scheme of things.

Consequently, here is a possible way to pray: "Answer our prayers today, Holy Presence, as we answer the prayers of those near us." It parallels the Our Father, of course: "Forgive us our trespasses, as we forgive those who trespass against us." In these biblical words we ask to be forgiven as we forgive. In the new prayer, we ask to be answered as we answer others' prayers.

I wonder: perhaps the new prayer might be helpful for those who puzzle how to respond to appeals for money, to help them be as generous as they can. "As you measure for others, so shall it be measured to you," said our Messiah. It comes to the same thing. As we judge, so we'll be judged. As we answer prayers, so our prayers will be answered. And after we have done what we can, we can feel a little better about the anguish that follows—because we are in solidarity with God's own anguish. Even if we were divine and perfect, we would not be without this anguish.

Sometimes my envelopes each get just a small amount. That is a little painful in itself; and there is anguish when some get no reply at all. But then it is time for my own prayer to God.

—From *Facing the Poor* by Patience O'Neil

Let God arise, and enemies be scattered,
And those who hate God be blown away like smoke,
As wax melts in the fire, so the haughty
Will lose heart before the Holy Face.

Why do you hide, my God?
Are you at my side, my God?

But let the righteous know the joy of freedom.
Let them exult before God's holy face.
Let them be jubilant with exultation,
And praise the God of justice and compassion.

Why do you hide, my God?
Are you at my side, my God?

Sing out to God, sing praises to God's name;
Lift up a song to God who rides the clouds.
God's name is high and royal in the heavens,
Come, dance in the royal court: the earth is God's.

Why do you hide, my God?
Are you at my side, my God?

A parent of the homeless and the stranger,
Protector of the widows and the poor
Is God who leads the prisoners out to freedom,
And gives the desolate a dwelling place.

Why do you hide, my God?
Are you at my side, my God?

PRACTICE
FOR
TODAY

Infinitely Resourceful Creator–Spirit,
teach me today to have faith in your plan
for me and my world.
Give me patience to live with things as they are.
And please teach me to walk in the beauty
that surrounds me in such abundance.

MANTRA

Why do you hide, my God?
Are you at my side, my God? ❑

I Am At Sea

My lostness shines like a beacon to your caring heart.
I am never alone,
least of all when things go wrong.

MINDFULNESS

Though I seem to have energy for nothing,
yet I will rejoice in God,
Though I seem at sea, adrift, going nowhere,
yet I will exult in God,
for you, Holy One, have energy, you are not adrift.
Though things do not go right for me,
though I am, this moment,
moved by no compelling task or person,
though I wait in vain for the dawn,
yet I will rejoice in God,
for your ways, my God, are sure,
and your world-project is on the move
even in the quiet and gloom of my depression.

CENTERING

Unknown Ocean of Mystery,
Creative Communion of Wisdom, Joy, and Life,

I know that somewhere
white herons feed their excited young,
kingfishers catch fire, dragonflies draw flame.
Somewhere there is good laughter
and plenteous insight.
In many places and hearts, creativity blossoms
like a hillside of daffodils,
like immense schools of salmon,
like endless plains of wildebeest,
like bright brains giving birth
to dreams destined to come true,
like mothers bringing forth
wholly new human persons
with new eyes that will grasp things
differently and better.

So I will rejoice in God,
I will not give up on creation.
I have instead given up on despair, egotism, and death.
I will choose to side with you, God of Life,
praying that my share of it is growing apace,
however much it may seem otherwise.

WORDS OF JESUS I am the light of the world. Whoever follows me will never walk in darkness but will have the light of life.

—*John 8:12*

FROM ANOTHER FAITH Blessed is the place and the dwelling
and the village and the city
and the heart
and the mountain and hermitage and cave
and the valley and the land
and the ocean and the island and the meadow
where mention of God has been made,
and the praise of God glorified.

—*Baha 'U' Lla'h, Nineteenth Century*

MEDITATION What a gift to anyone who seeks to be a person of prayer is the Good News that the Spirit can take our tears, our groans and sighs and weave them into words that delight the heart of God. At the death of someone

104

close to us, at the bedside of a sick child, or when we have accomplished something wonderful or fallen in love, we want to pray—but find that there are no words that can express to God the feelings of those sacred moments. Take heart and be glad, for it is at those times of great emotion that the Spirit makes music of great beauty from the deep stirrings of our hearts.

And not only at times of great emotion, but day in and day out, awake and asleep, the Spirit of the Holy is the Perpetual Pray-er within the sacred chapel of each of our hearts. This presence, however, does not excuse us from our efforts to pray and to make our prayers as full of love and devotion as possible. Nor does it grant us a dispensation from daily prayer.

Rather, such knowledge should challenge us to pray even more earnestly since we need no longer worry that God finds our prayers to be boring or a numbed collection of distractions and daydreams. In fact, those efforts can not only more fully align us to the Spirit, they allow our prayer to arise from the core, the very ground, of our being, where the Spirit resides. Moreover, because we are in touch with the Spirit, our prayers tend to be lighter, less weighed down by the gravity of our concerns. And since we take ourselves less seriously, our prayers rise more freely to God.

—from *The Pilgrim's Almanac* by Edward Hays

PRAYING WITH PSALM 102

Hear my prayer, Great God of All,
Let my cry for help reach your ears.
Do not turn your face from me
For I am deep in trouble.

You know my every pain and fear,
I thank you for your presence here.

For my days are disappearing like smoke,
My bones like ancient logs smoulder,
Even my heart is like the scorched grass
And the strength of my soul has gone.

You know my every pain and fear,
I thank you for your presence here.

PRACTICE
FOR
TODAY

Creative Communion of Wisdom,
make me wise enough today to escape my cocoon,
for life is short.
Let my days of colorful dancing delight all creation
and let my prayers rise freely to you this day.

MANTRA

You know my every pain and fear,
I thank you for your presence here.

A BUTTERFLY'S BEATITUDE

I leap into the sunshine,
I dance across the air,
I glorify the afternoon
And ridicule despair,
My wings a sunny yellow
Or wild design of gold,
I hint of hope for all the things
That prophets have foretold.

I know, dear God, my message
Seems trivial and droll,
Because I'm a lighthearted bug
Some think I have no soul.
But beauty goes with fairness
And justice as a boon,
So dancing joy implies the hope
For justice late and soon.

Amazing grace and beauty—
With justice—I will sing,
Though I am just another bug,
I proudly do my thing.
O Wondrous God of color,
Receive my thanks, I pray,
That I can have so rich a role
Though I live for but a day.

Be My Rock

The journey to my own center starts where I am:
at my truth, at my body-soul, at my skin.
I'll take just a moment for silence before I begin.

MINDFULNESS

Believing soul,
what makes you think God is forgiving?
What makes you think the Divine Being
—assuming there is One—cares about you?
Skeptical inquirer,
what makes you so sure
that there is no hell fire threatening you,
no Omnipotent Absurdity
sitting on heaven's throne?

CENTERING

The world around us
is far more violent than you really know:
There are torturers,
there are humans with diabolical aims,
there are diseases more horrible
than any parenting God could have designed,
animal behaviors more grotesque

and violent and irrational
than any benevolent "Mother Nature"
would have invented.

Hold on!
Does the world you know allow such doubts?
Might there be questions that may not be asked?
There can be and are.
In that theoretical world
where all questions may be asked
there is no room for real pain,
for absurd accidents,
for colossal blessing, for over-awing wonder—
like the speed of light, like the cosmos afire,
like the magnetism and ecstasy of love,
like the baffling wonder of animals and insects,
like the astonishing nobility of some human hearts,
like the cruelty of some lost souls.

But given the world we have,
at some point we cover our mouth with our hand,
we ask no more questions,
we are stumped.
And we go on with life in uncomplaining awe
because we are a part of the mystery that mystifies us.
We are not outside of it
where a question could be asked and answered.
We are inside, deep inside, the mystery.

WORDS
OF JESUS Blest are those who have not seen, but yet have believed.
—*John 20:29*

FROM
ANOTHER
FAITH Praise to God who alone is praiseworthy,
Praise to God for generosity and care,
Praise to God's power and goodness,
Praise to God's wisdom and knowledge.

O God, grant me light for my heart
and light for my tomb,
light in my hearing and light in my sight,
light for my flesh, my blood and my bones,

light in front of me, light behind me,
light to my right, light to my left,
light above and light below.
—*Abu Hamid Al-Ghazali, Fifth-Century Muslim Mystic*

What is the human condition? We look at life through color-distorting and shape-distorting glasses, but we don't realize we have the glasses on. We are wounded and handicapped: but deny it's true. In God's eyes we must appear to be belovedly clownish, with oversized eyes ("I's") and awkward feet and hands. At insightful times we seem to ourselves to be in a world of astonishing wonders and grotesque freaks: a circus universe.

So we need much more laughter. Relax. You're at the circus. In fact, you're a clown IN the circus. And we need others—to be our audience. Only in people's loving laughter we can properly estimate ourselves.

We have more than a few distorted "convictions," conceptual burlesques, and mental caricatures. We often hobble along like clowns wearing useless spectacles, balancing heavy halos on our heads. And we are funny mostly because what is funniest about clowns is their seeming conviction that they are normal. They make you smile; then they wonder why you're amused—which only makes you smile the more.

Be my rock, O God, my rock of refuge,
A strong fortress, where I can feel safe.
Rescue me, my Helper, from the wicked
And from the grasp of the cruel and unjust.

Behold me, God, before your holy face,
Give me your light, your healing, and your grace.

For you, dear God, are hope and trust and caring,
I've leaned upon you from my day of birth.
You took me from my very mother's womb
And from my youth I've learned to sing your praise.

Behold me, God, before your holy face,
Give me your light, your healing, and your grace.

Praiseworthy God, help me today to be among those
blessed who refuse to endure bad times in isolated silence,
for I will then find strength in the mystery of solidarity.
Let me walk in your Light this day.

Behold me, God, before your holy face,
Give me your light, your healing, and your grace.

TO LIGHTEN YOUR HEART

SONNET OF A CENTIPEDE

Across the sands a weary path I tread,
Life is not soft for me, it's not a cinch,
Like ships of old with many oars outspread
I move a hundred legs to walk an inch.

Some might have thought so many legs a boon,
Helping me move like lightning. It's not true.
More is not better, big is not opportune:
Sometimes I wish I had just four or two.

Still I believe my footsteps do make sense:
My role may be to clown and to amuse,
Giving a hint of your magnificence,
Grateful at least I don't have to wear shoes.

Oh, how I love to run barefoot through sand
Feeling a hundred thrills. Dear God, that's grand!

How Shall
I Forgive?

I am alone here before my enemies,
backed by my friends and family,
aware of the awesome presence of God,
loving, wise, compassionate, and dynamic.

MINDFULNESS

Dear God,
how shall we forgive those
who have sinned cruelly against us,
or pardon all trespasses, all bad will?
We know "whose sins we shall forgive,
they are forgiven"—
but how can we learn to forgive?

CENTERING

Should we begin by counting blessings:
the gifts we have received in such rich measure,
the precious persons, the precious days,
the exceeding wealth of life and promise
in which we share,
gifts as rich as gold, frankincense and myrrh,
rich enough for royalty?
In such a gracious world,

how can we not be gracious?
So we do pray to say: Forgiveness to our debtors!
Glory to our enemies!
so that all our own debts may be forgiven,
and our own anger be transformed.

May all our enemies thrive, prosper,
and enjoy this lovely earth.
They have enough regrets;
need they also regret they injured us?
They most probably "know not what they do."
We wish them—and ourselves—pardon, and joy.

WORDS
OF JESUS Peter said to Jesus, "If someone sins against me,
how often should I forgive? As many as seven times?"
Jesus answered,
"You must forgive seventy times seven times."
—Matthew 18:21–22

FROM
ANOTHER
FAITH Great Spirit Grandfather,
Everywhere I look,
the faces of living things are so alike
as they gently come up out of the Earth!
Guide your children
so they may turn their faces to the wind
and walk the good road
to the Day of Quiet.

Great Spirit Grandfather,
give us eyes to see.
Enlighten our way
so we may understand this:
to walk softly on the earth—
for we are relatives to all that is.
—Sioux Prayer

MEDITATION What seemed to anger Jesus of Nazareth? Hypocrisy
probably comes first, hypocrisy linked with the exploita-
tion of the faith of simple folk (they lay heavy burdens on
people's backs and will not move one finger to help
them). Cheating the poor was another vice that infuriated
him (You have made the house of prayer into a den of

thieves). Snobbery was another (Get thee behind me, Satan; you do not side with God...). Finally, arrogant judgments angered him (Let the one without sin cast the first stone). Most of these offenses could also be called injustice. Each offense, rather than simply breaking a rule, also wronged or belittled someone.

However, in the gospel episodes, when there is question of injustice against himself, Jesus seems to have been pretty stoical. Struck in the face once, he protested—but gently. The gospel stories do not, of course, tell us very much about Jesus himself—but rather tell about a community of his followers many years after his death, and what that community had remembered from his life and applied to themselves. Jesus may actually have been angry many more times than are recorded. If it was injustice that particularly angered him, he certainly was often angry—since it existed all around him.

Certainly one "virtue" that is an important one for us today is anger. Aquinas says that a person "sins" who is not angry in the presence of injustice; and that seems to state the truth simply and clearly. Anger is therefore sometimes a virtue, and it is the appropriate response to injustice.

Take pity on me, God, in your great heart,
Forgive my sins as I confess to thee,
Come, wash me thoroughly from all my faults,
And of my soul's burden, set me free.

I'm far from perfect in your sight,
Give me strength to set things right.

For I admit my faults, my shame and guilt,
And all I've done is here before my eyes,
Against your holiness I've set my face,
And chose to do what's selfish and unwise.

I'm far from perfect in your sight,
Give me strength to set things right.

A clean heart can thou make for me, O God?
A steadfast spirit build for me within?

Still hold me here before your holy face?
A larger life within my soul begin?

I'm far from perfect in your sight,
Give me strength to set things right.

Give back to me the shelter of your wing,
Your quiet presence with me all my days,
And when you open up my lips to sing,
My mouth shall all my life proclaim your praise.

I'm far from perfect in your sight,
Give me strength to set things right.

You take no pleasure in pure sacrifice;
You are not pleased by gifts of smoke and ash,
But love the humble seeker without pride;
An honest, contrite heart is all you ask.

I'm far from perfect in your sight,
Give me strength to set things right.

Take pity on me, God, in your great heart.
Forgive my sins as I confess to thee.
Come, wash me thoroughly from all my faults,
And of my soul's burden, set me free.

I'm far from perfect in your sight,
Give me strength to set things right.

PRACTICE FOR TODAY   God, Loving, Wise, and Compassionate, help me today to withhold judgment about offenders, assuming that such cases have mitigating circumstances. Deep in my heart I know that they always do. Help me to be angry about injustice, but to forgive those who sin against me seventy times seven times.

MANTRA   I'm far from perfect in your sight,
Give me strength to set things right. ❏

Beyond Words

See me before you, within you,
Nothing of mine unseen by you,
Yet nothing of you seen by me:
Darkness meeting Light.

MINDFULNESS

My life is an open book before you, Holy God,
there is nothing I can—or care to—hide.
In the first chapter are my spoken prayers.
I use words like: Welcome. . . Look. . . Ah. . . Your way. . .
Let it be. . . Thanks. . . Ready. . .

CENTERING

In the second chapter are my life's actions.
Here's where my strongest prayers start, meta-verbally,
as you "see" these prayers acted out in my life:
where and how I choose to live,
how I deal with each day's failures and successes,
how my heart goes out or stays away,
how, in the end, I send out my heart,
how I give time to one thing and not to another,
how I work, what I choose to do for work,
how I love, what I love,

how I deal with the inevitable,
where I give time or choose not to give time,
how lightheartedly I live, how largehearted I am,
how patient with myself, how forgiving;
So all that I am and do—speak eloquently to you
whether I want them to or not.
These are the prayers you always hear, my truest prayers.

In the third and last chapter of my life book,
you answer my prayers:
with my heart's beat—by which you give me life,
with my gradual aging—
by which you guide me toward you,
with the love of loved ones—by which you empower me,
with the presence of danger—
by which you ask my surrender,
with the presence of beauty—
by which you make promises,
with the flowers, with birdsong, with light and warmth,
and with so much more.
With all these things you speak to me
in the still-growing last chapter of the book of my life.

WORDS OF JESUS

Everyone to whom much is given, of them much will be required.   —*Luke 12:48*

FROM ANOTHER FAITH

O God, creator of our homeland,
earth, trees, animals and humans—
all that is honors you.
Drums beat it out,
people sing it,
and dance with noisy pleasure:
You are God.

—*Ashanti Prayer*

MEDITATION

We should not stop at words in our prayer life.
Touching your heart can say "Thanks."
Lighting a candle can say "You're here."
Hand over mouth can mean "You're beyond."
Nodding your head can say "Your way is best."
But you don't have to add words: the gesture will do.

Smiling at an enemy can say "You care."
Writing a difficult letter, visiting a difficult patient,
taking the last place, can say
"I believe, help thou my unbelief."
Enjoying a taste of wine can occasion a prayerful wink
or a savoring moment with God, beyond words.
The irresistible hug, the impromptu skip-step,
the affectionate touch can say "Alleluia."
If it delights us, it delights our Companioning God.
Laugh together. It's a heavenly moment—beyond words.

Let us make a joyful noise,
Celebrate our Rock of Trust,
Let us lift our hearts in a joyous song,
Ever sing to God we must.

All that I am and do
Speak constantly to you.

From the farthest depths of the earth
To the highest peaks in the air,
All is safe in the hands of a Sheltering Power
And she gives it perfect care.

All that I am and do
Speak constantly to you.

All the ocean deeps and floors,
All the mountains under the sea,
All was formed like clay in the potter's hands
And he gives it to you and me.

All that I am and do
Speak constantly to you.

O Come, give worship, dance and song,
Let us honor that Love Alive!
And a shepherding hand will guide us straight
To the valley where we can thrive.

All that I am and do
Speak constantly to you.

Though there's sorrow in our hearts,
And a painful path to trod,

Solidarity with all of Earth
Can unite us with our God.

All that I am and do
Speak constantly to you.

PRACTICE
FOR
TODAY Today, Holy God, help me to relax, remembering that all of life is a prayer—sometimes explicit, usually implicit.

MANTRA All that I am and do
Speak constantly to you.

GNIGHT PRAYER OF A GNAT

A gnat like me should gnot be singing psalms,
Or say a word,
It takes a swarm of gnats just to be seen,
Much less be heard.
Gno God will gnotice prayers from just one gnat:
The thought's absurd.

So I'll give up what gnormal prayers I'd say,
Life is too brief,
In solidarity with gnats worldwide
I'll state my grief:
Please God, gnats gneed more hope,
Less disbelief.

We can't believe we're on our way gnowhere,
It makes gno sense.
We're tiny, yet too gnoble to despair,
We're gnot that dense:
So every gnight we give ourselves to prayer,
And providence.

Holy Mystery

You alone know my name,
a name that includes all that I really am
and so much of that is unknown to me.
Call me by my name. Here I am.

MINDFULNESS

Holy Mystery,
Inexhaustible Source of Being
and of what should be
and of what we hope will be,
when I turn away from sorrow
and poverty, disfigurement, and disease,
and declare I'll have no part of it,
flare up within me
with persistent light and winning heat,
and draw something better out of me.

CENTERING

When I will not face life as it is:
a colossal circus of all that is awesome
—unimaginable wonders and perplexing freaks,
with clowns bridging the gap—

and I choose the more manageable milieu of the familiar
and the illusory,
give me new eyes, new ears, and a new heart,
one large enough for your ever-surprising reality.

When I prefer not to face death,
but choose to approach it backwards,
resting in what's past, swimming in memories,
eating only the stale bread of the traditional
and predictable,
sing me a siren song of desire for you
where you may ultimately be found and known:
in the future.

WORDS
OF JESUS **W**hat will it profit you if you gain the whole world
but end up losing your own self?

—Luke 9:25

FROM
ANOTHER
FAITH **G**randfather!
Look at our brokenness.
We know that in all creation
Only the human family has strayed from the Sacred Way.
We know that we are the ones who are divided.
And we are the ones
who must come back together
to walk again the Sacred Way.
Grandfather, Sacred One,
teach us love, compassion, and honor
that we may heal the earth
And heal each other.

—Ojibway Prayer

MEDITATION **T**he heart of this world's real absurdity is not so much in
the death and suffering we all abhor but in the astonishing life we have. Absurdity lies not in the defeats of
hope but in the victories we almost everywhere observe:
lovers discovering each other, a blazing sun-star giving almost immeasurable light and heat, everything on earth
growing, moving about purposefully, finding so much
that is joy-giving. These victories are astonishing partly

because they need not exist at all and are absurdly improbable in themselves.

There's the crucial absurdity. That some of these victories turn into defeats compounds the mystery but does not swamp it: the grace of the world abounds more than does its dis-grace, pain, or encroaching non-being. It is tunnel vision to call the pain absurd when the grace of joy in every created thing is colossally more absurd. There is no reality that could be "absurd" once you realize this (except in the abstract world of mathematics)—since there is nothing that is not already beyond absurdity.

My God, you are my shield and my protection,
The thought of you gives harbor to my soul,
And when my head's bowed down for any reason,
You lift my face and I can see the morning.

O Wisdom, Energy, Companion, Friend,
Stay with me through the ages without end.

All day with awe I visit with you freely.
At night I sleep because you hold me safe,
And I awaken still within your caring,
And offer praise to you in whom I trust.

O Wisdom, Energy, Companion, Friend,
Stay with me through the ages without end.

I shall not be afraid of any danger,
No matter who shall try to make me fear,
For you, my shield, my god, and my protection,
Do stand beside me all the night and day.

O Wisdom, Energy, Companion, Friend,
Stay with me through the ages without end.

Holy Mystery, Inexhaustible Source of Being,
today in the circle of my friends, and with your help,
I will stretch toward the wisdom of considering carefully
the opinions of those I most disagree with.
Let me sing and dance and beat drums today
with noisy pleasure because you are God.

O Wisdom, Energy, Companion, Friend,
Stay with me through the ages without end.

THE TURTLE'S THANKSGIVING

Dear God, amid life's battle I give thanks
Our forebears once evolved to walking tanks,
Tough-skinned as any buffalo or yak,
On land or sea safe-havened from attack.

We systematically call all things cursed:
Four-footed, two-footed, wing'd: which one is worst?
All but our turtle clan we shall distrust,
None is a friend and fear them all we must.

Still we have need of you, God of the Skies,
Give us this day, will you, our daily flies?
And please forgive our trespasses as well
Even if we won't come out of our shell!

Ah, what a shame that the world is thus,
Dangerous, warring, full of hatred-plus,
I beg, dear God, no worse things come to be—
And everyone hides in safety shells like me.

I Ask
the Impossible

All-but-unknowable God,
I will rest in what I know:
my body-self, my breath, my heartbeat,
and my need of you.

MINDFULNESS

May I ask the impossible?
Come, make it happen!
May this whole earthly family of mine,
Heart-gathering God,
be swept together somehow,
to where each name is called,
to where each and all hear the rest say, "Welcome!"
to where no one hides a face or conceals a wound,
to where all pain is turned to joy and meaning,
to where all gaps in the human dance are closed
and no one misses a beat anymore,
finding our way to that impossible place
of constant care and authentic connection:
Yourself. Impossible?
No. It is your will.
But it will take time.

CENTERING

Meanwhile, you are everywhere in the river of being,
and especially in our relationships, personal and social.
Help us take down the barriers between us:
the classism that isolates the hated rich
and the hated poor,
the racism that exaggerates difference
and distinguishes ins from outs,
the religious differences that emphasize words
over their meaning,
the language differences that marginalize large groups
on illusory grounds,
the national boundaries that protect privilege
and drain away energy.
Come, Saving God,
and establish your presence on the earth.
Come quickly.

WORDS OF JESUS   Where your treasure is, there will your heart be also.

—Luke 12:34

FROM ANOTHER FAITH   I speak with reverence in the presence
of the Great Parent God:
and give you grateful thanks
for enabling me to live this day,
from dawn to dusk,
in obedience to the ways of your spirit.

—Shinto Prayer

MEDITATION   Here's a story almost impossible to believe.

Once upon a time there was Wisdom. This was before the world existed, before birds sang in the trees, before humans walked the earth. And Wisdom was not alone, but had wonderful companions, playmates, and conSpiritors. Energy was one. Caringness was another. So wonderful was the companionship of these three—Wisdom, Energy, and Caringness—that they were always in and out of each other: Wisdom was Energetic, Energy was Caring, Caringness was Wise. In some ways the three were really one because they were never apart. In other ways they were three because they were always interacting.

Today we would call these three companions "God." They were also the Supreme Being—since nothing but they existed. But the best name for them might be "Divine Communion" since they were divine, and together, and in union with each other: Caringness, Wisdom, Energy: the Holiest Communion, our Creator.

Our Creator? Yes. It was the Communioning Threesome that, in a loving, energetic, and wise decision, chose to create this world, this galaxy we live in made up of stars and planets, and the whole immense cosmos we can see in the night sky—of uncountable glimmering, distant galaxies—with most of the millions of inhabitable planets probably filled, like the earth, with life.

Everything about this is mysterious. but one thing we can be sure of: our life is filled to overflowing with caringness, energy, and intelligibility. In fact, it is because this is true that we know about our Creator: that our parenting Divine Communion is Caringness, Energy, and Wisdom—because these three qualities are found everywhere in our world, a world covered with the fingerprints of their maker. Who figured this out? The religious detectives known as theologians, philosophers, and prophets.

It is they who tell us this story, almost impossible to believe. Once upon a time there was Inexhaustible Wisdom. And Wisdom was not alone, but had wonderful companions, playmates, and conSpiritors. Limitless Energy was one. Infinite Caringness was another.

In these three we live and move today, and have our own mysterious being.

Let us praise God.

Praise God in the sanctuary!
Praise God in the cemetery!
Praise God for the starry sky!
Praise God for the butterfly!

Praise God for colossal deeds,
for slugs and for centipedes!
Praise God with sounding cymbals!

Praise God with threads and thimbles!

Praise God in mosques and synagogues,
In temples, shrines, and churches!
Praise God in doubting atheists,
and everyone who searches!

On some bright day or darkling night
While brilliant star fires glisten,
Look! Everything is praising God!
It's happening! Just listen!

PRACTICE FOR TODAY Heart-Gathering God, may I be blessed enough today to never despair of hoping for "the impossible," because you've done more than that already.

MANTRA Praise He Who Is, Praise God!
Praise She Who Is, Praise God!

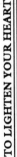

A CRICKET'S CANTICLE

Look down, dear God, I'm hiding in the grass
Playing my violin from dawn to night,
A tiny sound and badly out of tune,
But good enough for Mother Earth's delight.

I have to laugh, just listening to myself,
And then I jump to show I'm full of song.
I trust, Great God, you're cheered up by my tunes
Whenever you are sad and things go wrong.

I'm cheerful for the sun that warms my back,
I'm thankful for the music of my days,
So I will play my fiddle all my life,
Rejoicing in the comfort of your gaze.

Of Related Interest...

Psalm Services for Group Prayer

William Cleary

The ancient psalms of David form the basis for half the prayer services in this book. The other half features original psalms by the author.

ISBN: 0-89622-526-7, 96 pp, $9.95

Psalm Services for Parish Meetings

William Cleary

Cleary offers prayer services for otherwise ordinary meeting times, using the scriptural book of psalms and poetic psalms that he has written.

ISBN: 0-89622-510-0, 96 pp, $9.95

Weekly Prayer Services for Parish Meetings
Lectionary-Based for Year C

Marliss Rogers, Editor

Each of the 50 prayer services in this book follows a selected reading for each of the Sundays of the liturgical year (except Holy Week and the Sunday after Christmas).

ISBN: 0-89622-599-2, 112 pp, $12.95

Gathering Prayer

Debra Hintz

Thirty-five Scripture-based prayer services are offered here for church pastors and leaders.

ISBN: 0-89622-296-9, 80 pp, $9.95

Prayer Services for Parish Meetings

Debra Hintz

This book of 40 prayer services gives leaders the necessary means to begin small or large group meetings in a prayerful manner.

ISBN: 0-89622-170-9, 96 pp, $9.95

Available at religious bookstores or from

TWENTY-THIRD PUBLICATIONS

P.O. Box 180 • Mystic, CT 06355

1-800-321-0411